Staying True
in a World of Lies

Practical Models of Integrity
for Women in the Workplace

Julie-Allyson Ieron

⊕ CHRISTIAN PUBLICATIONS, INC.
CAMP HILL, PENNSYLVANIA

CHRISTIAN PUBLICATIONS, INC.

3825 Hartzdale Drive, Camp Hill, PA 17011
www.christianpublications.com

Staying True in a World of Lies
ISBN: 0-88965-205-8
© 2002 by Julie-Allyson Ieron
All rights reserved
Printed in the United States of America

02   03   04   05   06   5   4   3   2   1

Dedication

I offer this book, in gratitude, first to my mom
and then to all of the other women who have shown
me by their examples how to conduct myself in my career
as a woman of God. Ladies (you know who you are), I
want you to know how much I love and appreciate you!

Contents

Acknowledgments

This project would not have been possible without the candid and honest comments of the following women: Ann*, Bev, Carla, Carrie*, Christina*, Eileen, Elizabeth*, Holly, Jean*, Jenny, Joan, Jodi, JoyAnn, Lori, Mary*, Rene and Tammy. My dear friends, I cannot thank you enough—for the awesome examples you have been to me and for your willingness to open your lives to everyone who will read this book.

To my parents, John and Joyce Ieron, your continued patience with me and prayers for me throughout the writing of yet another book qualify you for another extra jewel in your heavenly crown.

To my friend and former editor Don Anderson, thank you for searching your personal library to provide me with dozens of resources published over the years on the life of Queen Esther.

To my publishers, especially to Managing Editor David Fessenden who believed in this project since it was just an idea in my own mind, to former Editorial Director George McPeek who worked out all the arrangements to make this book possible, to my talented editor Laurie Gustafson, to the artist Jerry Dorris who designed a cover that made you pick this book off the shelf and to the entire marketing team who saw to it that this book would make it into your hands—to each of you my undying gratitude for your partnership in the mission.

Finally, for you, my dear reader, I offer a prayer of thanksgiving that you've chosen to spend moments of your busy life reading what I've written. It is my prayer that this book will challenge you, as it has me, to put into practice the Scripture verse that tells us: "And whatever you do, whether in word or deed, do it all in the name of the Lord Jesus, giving thanks to God the Father through him" (Colossians 3:17).

*Because these women chose to be especially candid in their comments, they asked to be identified with pseudonyms.

Prologue

Jodi's Story: The Character of a Culture

For one school year in the early 1990s I taught English in China at a top science and technology university. There I encountered a situation that distilled the issues of integrity for me.

As an English professor, I was required to give my students both writing assignments and exams. I had several classes, from basic to advanced. In my advanced class, I had a favorite student. He always did a good job on class work and was developing a good command of the English language. On one assignment he did an especially good job. I graded the paper and gave it an A. Then, while I was giving an exam in my basic level class, I picked up a book and opened to a page at random. I recognized what I was reading—it was his paper, verbatim. He had plagiarized it.

The worst part is that in China plagiarism isn't considered wrong or dishonest. My values were butting heads with the culture of the country in which I was working.

When the student came to class the next time, I took him into another room and showed him the book. He took responsibility and said to me, "I am so sorry." I asked him why he did it. He said he was swamped and didn't have time to do the paper. I told him I would have rather he had come to me and told me he was swamped. I explained that plagiarism is wrong, no matter what the culture says.

The issue then was: what should be the penalty for this dishonesty? He was afraid I would report him, but I told him I wouldn't. Instead, he received an F for that assignment, but I told him if he kept coming to class and doing his work he could continue his studies. He asked why I would do that. Without a second thought, I replied with one word: grace.

1

In one sense you must put other people on the spot with what you know is right. And you have to make decisions about things that can be detrimental to them. But I had prayed about it. I knew this was the way to go. We could all use some grace.

"Simply let your 'Yes' be 'Yes,' and your 'No,' 'No'; anything beyond this comes from the evil one." (Matthew 5:37)

Over the course of her life Madeleine Albright was a refugee from Hitler, an escapee from communism, a student who paid for her studies by working menial-labor jobs, a wife and mother, a party to an unwanted divorce, a scholar, a professor, a political underling, an envoy, and for much of the 1990s the chief diplomat of the United States.[1]

In her highly visible role as Secretary of State, Madeleine developed a distinctive style that has made her recognizable on sight. She wears carefully selected brooches (for example, she wore one that features two doves of peace when meeting with Palestinian leaders), brightly colored scarves, even a black cowboy hat when appropriate. She doesn't wear navy pinstriped pants suits with red ties or try to fit in with "the guys." She looks and acts like a woman, and is still able to remain tough on the issues of peace and human rights her bosses hired her to protect.

Dr. Albright worked long years to achieve a delicate balance between being taken seriously in the professional world and not losing sight of the distinctive qualities that make her a woman. One of her biographers, Ann Blackman, describes Albright's dilemma by explaining that the Secretary tried "to master the precarious dance between family and job, vocation and avocation."[2]

Apparently, the Secretary has succeeded in achieving a measure of this precarious balance. According to Blackman, "President Clinton realized that he had in [Dr. Albright] a dazzling speaker with unquestioned loyalty to the people she served, a natural politico who could handle the press while giving him credit for American foreign policy decisions and not seek acclaim for herself."[3] Yet Blackman describes her as "a woman who cares deeply for her daughters and family, a generous friend, a homemaker turned politician turned diplomat, who thrives on friendships with women and enjoys the company of men."[4]

This is a book about the very dilemma Dr. Albright has faced: the dilemma you and I, as women, face every day. Because, truth be told, it is a complex balance, one we are apt to strike one day and topple the next.

Our dilemma is not just one of culturally accepted norms, but one that meets us at the heart of our faith. For not only are we seeking to please professional colleagues and superiors, not only are we seeking to serve the needs of our families, but as women of faith we are also working hardest at pleasing our Master, Jesus Christ. We recognize that if we please all others but fail to meet Christ's expectations of us, we have failed in all that ultimately matters.

Just the Facts

This is not a book that argues whether or not women ought to work outside the home. Look around you. It is a given that, in nearly every culture on earth, we women are in the workplace. Maybe not for every season of life, but for some of the seasons of life. I'm thirty-something (never mind thirty-what) and single. I've been in the workforce since 1986. I've worked while pursuing a graduate degree. I've held management positions in secular corporations, Christian organizations and now my own company. I've been a writing and communications instructor in universities and in business settings. I've been, at times, my own sole supporter and at other times a contributing member of a family household.

As I write, I try to envision your circumstances. I try to imagine whether you are married or single, divorced or widowed; whether or not you have children; whether you are working to help put a roof over your head or pay your children's college bills, whether you are your household's primary supporter or provider of enjoyable extras. Maybe you've just joined the workforce; maybe you're returning to it after years of absence; maybe you've never left. Regardless of the particulars, you are a fellow woman who has asked many of the same questions I have asked. We are, in some sense, kindred spirits. We are companions on the journey toward pleasing our God and achieving His purposes in our spheres of influence.

The fact remains that we are women who both love Jesus Christ and who are playing increasingly powerful roles in the secular world. So, then, how are we to act? Are we to mimic our male colleagues by becoming as masculine as possible? Are we to be wishy-washy dishrags who never disagree with the men in our workplace? I don't find either of these extremes particularly compelling for ourselves or for the sake of the gospel of Jesus Christ that we represent. And I believe there has to be a better way, a balance point in which we remain true to our natures as women and yet succeed by making significant contributions in our spheres. Ideally, it would be a balance point similar to the one Madeleine Albright has found—one similar to the one Jodi found with her Chinese student. Finding that point together will be the goal of this book.

We Begin Our Search

As I do whenever I face a life issue, I have searched the Bible seeking to identify the tasks God saved for women to accomplish and to learn how Bible women were able to please Him.[5] In the pages of the Bible I found many examples of God-fearing women who had established themselves as credible, hard workers, whose integrity and character were beacons to the world around them. In particular, I focused my study on the life of the Persian Queen Esther, whom God used to bring deliverance to His people. Esther, as you will see as we look at her life together, rose to a position of unparalleled influence because of a sweet spirit, an inner beauty, an outward attractiveness and a humility tempered by steely determination.

Examples of other women of the Bible fill out the picture as well. Ruth shows us a loyalty that we would be wise to emulate; Mary, sister of Lazarus, shows us the heart of a listener; the prophetess Huldah shows us the power of credibility and wise counsel; Priscilla reminds us of the power of communication; Moses' mother Jochebed shows us the power of restraining ourselves and Judge Deborah models for us how to use our God-given responsibilities wisely and gently.

The character traits these women exhibit seem to converge in one jam-packed word: integrity. A simple definition of this complex concept is: "doing what we said we would, when we said we would, while never promising more than we can deliver."

I can't take credit for this concept. I first encountered it early in my career as a journalist when I was interviewing corporate CEO Sherm Swenson for a magazine profile article. Swenson, having seen a deficiency of this character trait in business school graduates, retired from a lucrative professional career to become an administrator at Bethel College in St. Paul, Minnesota. Sherm and his wife began to mentor a small group of business students each year, teaching them by word and by example to exhibit the character traits of honesty and integrity in their work lives. Sherm's constant refrain was "do what you say you'll do, when you said you'd do it." Since meeting Sherm I've never been able to get that refrain to stop playing in my mind. To him the concept of integrity includes an aspect of wholeness which allows us to approach life honorably, unencumbered by the baggage of guilt and remorse, unconcerned about carrying to their farthest limits any lies we've told. Even through our brief acquaintance, Sherm taught me that we establish for ourselves a good name by dealing fairly, justly and honestly with everyone we encounter.

Beyond Honesty

But integrity encompasses more than simply the idea of honesty or even the principle of being true to our word. These are just a surface understanding of the principle. Integrity is actually a brand of unity—a unity between what we say and what we do. These, taken together, make up the quality of our character.

Integrity means keeping confidences. It means maintaining trust and prizing trustworthiness. It means remaining true to the guiding principles (or ethics) we hold dear even when it might be detrimental to our career progress in the short-run— even when it would be easier to toss out our principles and conform to a culture of moral compasses that spin helplessly without establishing a true north. And integrity means living lives that would stand up to the most intense scrutiny, so that were our deeds and our thoughts shouted from the rooftop, we would have no reason to be ashamed.

From intensive research and firsthand observations on integrity as it plays out in the workplace (I've observed those who have it and those who don't), I've identified a dozen of the key traits or attributes that seem to characterize those who maintain and cultivate their integrity at work. These are attractiveness, grace, trustworthiness, loyalty, attentiveness, credibility, friendliness, sensitivity, prudence, wisdom, restraint and openness.

As George W. Bush prepared to assume the presidency in January 2001, I watched his cabinet appointees defend their credentials and their life choices before Senate confirmation committees. In these hearings, everything that could be uncovered was uncovered. One appointee was forced to withdraw her name because of a questionable financial arrangement which had occurred years before with a foreigner who was in this country illegally. Another appointee was forced to defend his principles—his Bible-driven, moral principles. He emerged blameless, and eventually his guiding principles, though called into question, did not disqualify him from service in the Senate's eyes.

It all reminds me of the principle the Apostle Peter stated: "Dear friends, I urge you, as aliens and strangers in the world, to . . . [l]ive such good lives among the pagans that, though they accuse you of doing wrong, they may see your good deeds and glorify God" (1 Peter 2:11-12). A few verses later, Peter tells his readers, "For what credit is there if, when you sin and are harshly treated, you endure it with patience? But if when you do what is right and suffer for it you patiently endure it, this finds favor with God" (1 Peter 2:20, NASB).

This is the lifestyle of integrity. I will not lie to you and say that it has no consequences in this fallen world. I will not tell you that making choices out of godly principles will ever come naturally or easily. And yet I submit to you that as a follower of Jesus Christ, this lifestyle must be our target, our ultimate goal.

I must warn you that one principle, above all others, will be foundational to this book. It is this: We cannot have ethics or solid moral character if we build on the shifting standard of what we choose to think is "right for each of us." The Bible is pretty clear on this subject: Right does not change depending on who we are and what our circumstances are on any given day. Right is always right. Wrong is always wrong.

The only unchanging standard of life is found in the principles of God's Word. It is a standard that worked when lived out millennia ago in Bible times (by the likes of Deborah, Esther,

Anna and others) and it works when lived out in this third millennium after Jesus Christ walked this earth.

Flesh and Blood Examples

OK, perhaps you're sold, as I am, upon maintaining character, integrity, godliness and womanliness in your work life, as well as in your home and church life. It sounds good in principle. But just how does it play out in everyday, twenty-first-century life? Is it an attainable goal or just another castle in the sky?

Once I identified the characteristics that God would have us exhibit as women, I looked for flesh-and-blood examples among the women I have met along the journey. They are few and far between, but they are out there, busily carrying out these principles in the workaday world. These women are professionals in higher education, administrators, attorneys, elected officials, journalists, beauty professionals, office workers, managers, consultants, business owners, head-hunters and more. They are twenty-something to sixty-something. Some are married; others are single. Some have children; others don't. Some have been believers in Christ all of their lives; others are just embarking on their journeys of faith. None of them is perfect, but all are striving toward consistency as they pursue a lifestyle of honorability. (For more information on the women mentioned in this book, see the Cast of Characters on page 203.)

Regardless of their life stages, these are women who have achieved a measure of success while staying true to their God-given callings. They are women of character, women I want to emulate. And so I introduce them to you, in the hopes that through their stories you will learn from their choices, as I have, to be a woman who stays true to her God and to her God-given nature, in a world of masks, of falsehoods, of lies.

Questions for Prayerful Consideration

1. At what stage of life do you find yourself today? To whom are you responsible at this time in your life?
2. In what areas have you experienced difficulty in balancing God's expectations of you with the world's expectations of you?
3. Who are some of the women whose examples you would like to emulate? Why?
4. What questions have you encountered as you've embarked on your professional life?
5. How do you want your coworkers, superiors and subordinates to view you? What will you do today to move toward that goal?

Endnotes

1. U.S. Secretary of State during Bill Clinton's presidency.
2. From *Seasons of Her Life* by Ann Blackman. Excerpt appears on the book's promotional web site at the address: http://www.seasonsofherlife.com/Book/Excerpts/excerpts.html.
3. Ibid.
4. Ibid.
5. I began by revisiting the research I had undertaken originally for my first book, *Names of Women of the Bible* (Moody Press, 1998).

Attractive in Spirit

And let the beauty of the LORD our God be upon us,
And establish the work of our hands for us;
Yes, establish the work of our hands.

(Psalm 90:17, NKJV)

My Own Story: A Lesson in Beauty

I never thought much about the external image I wanted to ·project to a watching world. Since my college years I had always risen early enough to dress not only comfortably and fashionably, but also to do "something" with my hair and apply a light layer of makeup. I did this not because I was trying to impress anyone else, but because it made me feel more comfortable, more unified, more like I was projecting on the outside what I was feeling on the inside. In the office, it made me feel more professional. In classes, it made me feel more prepared, less harried, less self-conscious. As a young university instructor, it made me feel more worthy of teaching a classroom full of inquiring minds.

All of this was somehow ingrained into my daily preparations. I hadn't given it a second thought until a colleague, who was also the wife of an inner-city pastor, asked me to speak to a women's seminar at her church on the subject of beauty. She said that she had been working with these women at succeeding in the workplace and she knew they lacked the ability to project an attractive professional image. After praying about it, she felt I might be able to help in that area.

So I went to work. I gathered the latest fashion tips; piled scarves, pins, hosiery and other accessories into a suitcase and prepared to address the group. But suddenly I felt vulnerable and unprepared to talk with those women about true beauty, which the wise writer of Proverbs says is more than something we can put onto our external bodies. "Charm is deceptive, and beauty is fleeting; but a woman who fears the LORD is to be praised" (Proverbs 31:30). So I turned to the story of one of the most beautiful women in the Bible—Esther, queen of Persia—for help in preparing these women to exude an attractive spirit.

That night I was able to help several women learn to accessorize their wardrobes; I showed them examples of clothing choices that would help them make lasting impressions of professionalism at work. But most importantly I told them the story of Esther, who rose from obscurity to become the most powerful woman in the most powerful empire on earth at that time.

I concluded my presentation with this charge: "God delivered His people from certain annihilation because one woman, Esther, made an outstanding first impression on a king. But Esther's example demonstrated that she was more than beautiful on the outside—she was a wise, thoughtful and discerning young woman. Regardless of my age or my looks, I want to be that beautiful on the inside. Don't you?"

Even today I don't believe we could find a better example to follow than that of young Esther, who packaged her inner beauty in the wrappings of external attractiveness.

I learned a new word today. Perhaps you've heard of it. The word is *womanfully*. Even my computer's word processor didn't recognize it, so don't feel self-conscious if you've yet to add it to your everyday vocabulary. What attracted me to this word was its dictionary definition. Here's the entry from The American Heritage Dictionary: "wom·an·ful·ly *adv.*: with the characteristic grace, strength, or purposefulness of a woman."

Actually, I learned two words today. There is a parallel word to this one. It is *manfully*. Its definition is: "Having or showing the bravery and resoluteness considered characteristic of a man."

These words bespeak the contrast that forms the basis for this book: Neither manfully nor womanfully speaks of power or weakness, superiority or inferiority. Instead the two speak of complementary contrasts: graceful strength in contrast with raw bravery; purposefulness in contrast with resoluteness. Both are needed in every arena of life, not the least of which is the workplace.

In most cases strength and bravery lead a circumstance to the same closure, as do purposefulness and resoluteness. Typically (though not without exception), women are more becoming, more womanful, when exhibiting graceful strength as opposed to brash bravado, when exhibiting steel-magnolia purposefulness (or determination) rather than impenetrable resoluteness.

Sadly, I have seen some female managers err on the side of conducting themselves manfully in the workplace. Perhaps without realizing it, the manager will begin to concede her distinctive feminine qualities as recompense for her success in a male-dominated world. Eventually, she settles so comfortably into the male hierarchy that she comes to look and act male. She dresses in dark business suits tailored for the male body and grooms herself sparsely, without the slightest nod toward femininity.

Once she has cast womanfulness aside, the woman's tendency is to take on the worst, most blatantly macho qualities—perhaps with the subconscious goal of proving to male counterparts just how tough she can be. At the extreme, I have seen women become impertinent, callous, verbally abusive, crude, indifferent and even downright obnoxious. In short, anything but womanly.

Is this metamorphosis a natural outgrowth of women assuming roles of leadership in the workplace? Is it a necessary evil to be endured? Or is there an alternative, a middle ground similar to that achieved by Madeleine Albright, who is one among many in the trailblazing generation for the modern woman?

In the last decade and a half, I have encountered a few female bosses and management colleagues who found the right mix. These are women who clothe themselves externally (as appropriate in their office settings) with business suits cut to enhance (but not exploit) a woman's distinctive curves. Their grooming is stylish and includes a light and attractive application of makeup. They are equally as careful as they pattern their all-important internal attractiveness. They clothe themselves with fragrantly appealing personalities. I would describe them as sometimes tough but always kind; as driven to succeed, but unwilling to sacrifice their innate distinctiveness for the sake of temporary advancement.

In a culture that is changing its expectations at breakneck speed, what does the new millennium professional woman look like—on the inside and on the outside?

On the Outside

The freedoms of the new millennium woman were hard won by women who came to the workplace in the 1960s and 1970s. Joan is one of those trailblazing women. A recently semiretired CPA who ran her own firm for several decades, Joan is recognized by colleagues, staffers and clients alike as a steely, determined, yet feminine woman.

She recalls one formative experience from her college years where she was often the only woman in her upper division business courses. "I was a senior, and I was up for the top accounting business award. The chief of the accounting division came to me and said, 'I just want to tell you that you're not going to get that award—no woman will ever get that award. So you can forget it.' " How did she handle that? "My dad used to say, 'What are you going to do—lie down and cry, or get up and go?' " So, unashamed of being an intelligent woman, perhaps even bolstered by this affront, Joan got up and moved on.

Upon graduation she had the opportunity to be the first female accountant at a major corporation, yet she declined. "I chose not to take it because I knew they were going to put me in a corner someplace and treat me as a token. Instead, I worked for a stock brokerage firm where they really put me to work. And I learned a lot in the process."

Joan is from the "old school" (as my mother calls it) and is still sold on the classic Madeleine Albright look for women in the workplace. "You can never go wrong by being dressed with dignity and professionalism," she says. Here's how she describes her own trademark look:

When I would go to IRS offices, to audits, to meetings, I never, ever wore a pantsuit. Even today, I always wear a skirted suit or a dress. I always look the part of being a woman, a professional woman. I try to make sure that I match from head to toe and that I look as professional as possible. I'm not saying that I have to be gaudy—I do like to wear gray because it goes with my hair—but I try to put my best foot forward.

For example, I spoke before the executive training branch of the Internal Revenue Service when they came to my city for a meeting. And the assistant district director who met me at the door remarked, "Joan, I knew I didn't have to worry about whether you would dress appropriately. You always dress professionally."

But dressing professionally for the generation that is emerging in today's workplace may look a little foreign to Joan. Those of us who are in that next wave, who are indebted to the sacrifices of Joan and trailblazers like her, now have more flexibility in creating our own professional identities, our own images in the workplace.

Sharon O'Malley, editor of *Work/Life Today* (a monthly newsletter about companies that help employees balance their careers with their personal lives), writes in an article posted on the *Working Woman* web site, "Workplace style has shifted away from the perfected coordinates of the dark-blue suit and toward the comfier call of khaki slacks." The shift to which she refers is the pendulum swing toward a style of dress known as "business casual," formerly an oxymoron—now more the norm than the exception.

Quoting one source as saying, "Women don't have to look like their male counterparts like they did in the '80s . . . they can be feminine," O'Malley advises readers to "dress like a woman," purchase "mix-and-match slacks, skirts, and blazers . . . use accent colors to spruce up the basic tans and blacks," and most of all, "dress to show respect and good taste." Like Joan, O'Malley advises women that when in doubt, it is always safest to err on the side of looking overly professional rather than overly casual.[1]

Nowhere is this shifting norm more apparent than in the nursing profession. Rene, a critical care nurse whose story is shared in Chapter 5, has seen the dress code in nursing move from "all white, all the time" to almost anything goes, depending on the setting.

> We are dressed in almost any color. Some nurses wear lab coats over street clothes. There are so many different roles in nursing that you may see nurses in scrubs or nurses in business suits. In critical care, we wear scrubs because it is more prudent for dealing with infectious diseases. Nevertheless, as nurses we dress and carry ourselves in such a way that when we walk into a patient's hospital room, there's no doubt that we are the nurses, the caregivers.

At the opposite end of the spectrum from Joan and other business-suited women of today is Lori, a twenty-something makeup artist who manages the makeup department for a large chain of salons. She chose her profession, after trying her hand at a few others, because, in her words, "I'm not just making someone look beautiful, I'm making her *feel* beautiful. I love seeing women's self-esteem rise. I get satisfaction from that."

She divides her time between the nuts and bolts of a management role and the hands-on artistic side of her profession, performing makeovers on women as part of their spa experience.

Lori gives the example of a female paramedic who came to her for advice on a look that would be practical but that would also keep her from looking like one of the guys. Lori gave this woman some of the same counsel she gives other professional women, especially those who work in an office setting.

> You want to look professional and polished. If you're too trendy, you might not be taken seriously by your clients or your coworkers. You want your makeup and your hairstyle to look updated but not trendy. You want people to see you and your features, not your makeup.
>
> Your whole look should match your makeup. Don't wear anything too sexy, but you don't have to wear a suit that makes you look boring. On the too sexy side are miniskirts, leather and low-cut tops. On the boring side is the look that is too classic. People will tend to think you're too out of touch to warrant a hearing.
>
> There are beautiful suits that are updated, suits that are what I call updated classic. Not stuffy, but fresh looking. If that's how you look, that's how you'll feel. Then people will notice that and pay attention to you.

On the Inside

But, as a remarkably grounded (if still young) believer in Jesus Christ, Lori is quick to point out that beauty and attractiveness are not skin deep. They are character traits we must cultivate on the inside if we expect them to show up on the outside. Lori says,

> Being a beautiful woman of integrity, I would say, is being someone who is honest, virtuous, puts others before herself and sees other people's needs. If you don't have honesty, wisdom, integrity, kindness, gentleness; if you don't put others before yourself and show love by being a good friend, you're not beautiful at all. How many times do you see someone who is physically beautiful but ugly on the inside? Yes, you can update yourself, but your outward beauty may fade away. A woman who fears the Lord—that's someone to look up to. The women I look up to aren't the most gorgeous; they're the ones who have Christ at the center of their lives.

Lori's mother, Eileen, an inside sales manager for a division of a large conglomerate, describes the inner beauty she tries to live out and also to instill in her daughter this way: "I want people to see Christ in my life, so I'm trying to live so that they see that what's inside me is a quiet and gentle spirit. Sometimes I fail—I'm human. But that's what I want to be on the inside: quiet and gentle."

Eileen's word choice comes straight out of Scripture. The Apostle Peter writes these instructions to women of faith:

> Your beauty should not come from outward adornment, such as braided hair and the wearing of gold jewelry and fine clothes. Instead, it should be that of your inner self, the unfading beauty of a

gentle and quiet spirit, which is of great worth in
God's sight. For this is the way the holy women of
the past who put their hope in God used to make
themselves beautiful. (1 Peter 3:3-5)

It's not that the outward things—such as having a fash-
ionable hairdo or attractive clothing or pretty jewelry—are
wrong; it's that these should not be the most important elements of our daily beauty regimens. We know from other
passages in the Bible that God examines our hearts—what is
on the inside. Underneath all of the external whitewashing
we do to make ourselves presentable to the outside world,
He sees our true selves—with all of our warts and all of our
shortcomings. He also sees in us the true, unfading beauty
that He created in our souls. It is that beauty women like
Eileen, Lori, Rene and Joan are working to cultivate daily.

Which brings us back to where we began this chapter: with a
woman who spent twelve months making herself beautiful on
the outside in preparation for her moment alone with the king
of Persia, but more crucially who spent a lifetime preparing
herself with an inner beauty, an attractiveness that made her
stand out from among all of the other magnificent beauties who
had been conscripted into the king's harem. Observe the way
Esther's experience is described:

Before a girl's turn came to go in to King
Xerxes, she had to complete twelve months of
beauty treatments prescribed for the women, six
months with oil of myrrh and six with perfumes
and cosmetics. . . .

When the turn came for Esther (the girl Mordecai had adopted, the daughter of his uncle Abihail) to go to the king, she asked for nothing other than what Hegai, the king's eunuch who was in charge of the harem, suggested. And Esther won the favor of everyone who saw her. She was taken to King Xerxes in the royal residence in the tenth month, the month of Tebeth, in the seventh year of his reign.

Now the king was attracted to Esther more than to any of the other women, and she won his favor and approval more than any of the other virgins. So he set a royal crown on her head and made her queen instead of Vashti. (Esther 2:12, 15-17)

I'd love to talk to Esther, because I really want to tap into her beauty secrets. If I could, I'd ask her what was going through her mind during those twelve long months of preparation. I'd ask what worried her. What excited her. I'd ask whether she enjoyed the pampering or whether it made her feel at least a little self-conscious. I'd ask where she found an inner quiet, a peaceful spirit in the hustle and bustle of harem life. I'd ask what made her think of asking the king's eunuch what would be most pleasing for her to bring with her when she went to the king. I'd ask if she looked at her reflection in a pond as she walked across the courtyard on her way to the king's chamber. I'd ask what she thought of her transformed self. And most of all I'd ask if she felt changed on the inside.

I suspect, and this is only conjecture, mind you, but I suspect that on the inside she was still the same sweet innocent girl who was brought along with the other young virgins into the harem all those months before. I draw this conclusion because the Bible's account tells us that she "won the favor of everyone who saw her" (2:15). And I think of Lori's words, that the most gorgeous women are those who have the Lord at the center of their lives. This girl of the Jewish culture and faith was enmeshed in the secular marketplace of the day—the household of a pagan king—yet, like Hebrew captives of another generation (Daniel and his three friends, Shadrach, Meshach and Abednego), her unblemished character caused her to rise to prominence, above the cream of all of the young people of that culture.

Clearly, although His name is never mentioned in the account of Esther's life, God was with her—blessing, protecting, directing and enabling her to earn the approval of all who encountered her, the mighty king included. Her inner beauty and her obvious dependence on the God of her ancestors won her acceptance in the royal courts.

Uniting the Interior and the Exterior

How can we cultivate inner beauty and a quiet and gentle spirit in a twenty-first-century world of technology, space travel and constant scientific inquiry? Our scenery, our backdrop may have changed from that of Esther's time, but the principle remains the same.

Perhaps this example will bring one more degree of clarity to our discussion of true beauty. Jodi, whose experience teaching English in China opened this book, offers this telling word picture:

> As a woman in the workplace, I want to exhibit gentle power—like the Bible women Abigail, Esther, Miriam and Deborah. These women weren't wimpy. They were princesses who had authority to go and to do what God was calling them to do. They did His work.
>
> Maybe this sounds a little silly, but it helps me to picture myself as one of the nobles in a king's court. I sit at the table with the other nobles. But I'm not dressed like the men. I am a woman, and I am dressed appropriately as a woman. When I go into battle, I don't do battle like the male nobles. I act in battle the way that is appropriate to the battle gear I wear.

When I was writing my first book, *Names of Women of the Bible*, I researched the meanings of the names of fifty-two of the women in the Bible. One of those women whose testimony I researched was Phoebe. I remember her well because her name means "radiant" in Greek. That seems to have been her personality, as well. I surmise that because when the Apostle Paul refers to Phoebe at the close of the book of Romans, he commends her to the believers in Rome as one who is a "sister," a "servant" and a "great help to many people" (Romans 16:1-2). Radiant Phoebe found a way to let that inner beauty of a gentle and quiet spirit shine through.

So Phoebe shows us, as did Esther generations before, that when God is with us—granting us His favor, His blessing, His approval, His worthiness to accomplish His work—an inner beauty will radiate from inside us. This radiance will outpace any fading beauty treatments we may give ourselves on the outside.

Questions for
Prayerful Consideration

1. How have I defined beauty in the past?
2. How can I make an effort to enhance my external attractiveness in ways that are appropriate for my workplace?
3. How has this study impacted my previous conceptions of beauty?
4. Who are the most beautiful women I have ever known? What can I learn from their examples?
5. What are three specific, practical ways I can work to exude the inner beauty of a gentle, quiet spirit?

Endnote

1. Sharon O'Malley. "Ready to Wear," www.workingwoman.com/wwn/article.jsp?contentId=5151.

Two

Full of Grace

Let your conversation be always full of grace, seasoned
with salt, so that you may know how to answer every-
one. (Colossians 4:6)

Holly's Story—Journalist Prizes Grace over Justice

Two young reporters—Brian and I—were hired the same
week. I had a college degree; he didn't. I had majored in
journalism; he had majored in music. Yet he was paid $15 a
week more than I. When I inquired "why," our boss explained that Brian was a guy and I was a girl.

Grace? I was furious. Yet I couldn't show it toward my
boss; I needed this job. So I took it out on Brian.

He would often ask me to go out for a burger during our
dinner hour; I would refuse. He would try to make small talk
in the newsroom; I would cut him off. Every time I looked at
him I saw dollar signs: fifteen of them!

One night he was stranded and needed a lift home. Since
he lived in my direction, I had no choice. Alone with him in
the car, I was a captive audience. He wasted no time in getting to the point. He said he couldn't apologize for his gender, and he couldn't apologize for our unequal treatment by
our boss. But he said he understood my feelings, acknowl-
edged that I was more qualified and he would very much like
to be my friend. He even offered to ask our boss to equalize
our pay—if the company wouldn't up my wages, then it
should decrease his . . . by $15.

We talked well into the night and I made a friend for life. What a lesson in grace for me! Brian left the newspaper to go back to school a few months later, and many years later I had worked my way up to my former boss's job.

Brian died tragically a couple of years later, but I will always thank God that our paths crossed, at least for a little while.

*I*n our "me first" generation, grace is a difficult concept to comprehend, and it is a difficult virtue to exude. We may say that a beautiful woman is graceful, but do we really mean that she is "full of grace"? More often, we mean she moves smoothly and elegantly; her gestures are agile and flowing; she is pleasant to behold.

Esther's manner and conduct in the king's court, both before and after she became queen, exuded a quiet grace in abundance.

One line in the biblical account, in particular, bears this out. When Esther was entrusted to Hegai, the keeper of the king's harem, the Scripture says, "The girl pleased him and won his favor" (Esther 2:9). Esther's inner beauty, coupled with her humility and grace, were the magnetic charges that drew Hegai's (and soon the king's) favor. These set her apart from the rest of the beautiful women. It is likely that many of the other women were vain, enamored with their own loveliness, preoccupied with an external, eye-catching brand of beauty.

Esther, instead, seems to have exuded a gentle gracefulness. She didn't spend time bemoaning her fate—a young captive woman taken (whether willingly or unwillingly, we do not know) to spend the rest of her life confined to the king's harem; a Hebrew woman forevermore at the mercy of a capricious pagan king. Instead, Esther was pleasing to be around. In fact, the king's servant was so delighted with the graceful girl that he was pleased to serve her—even before she became queen.

Grace contributed greatly to Esther's successful foray into the king's court. Similarly, grace is a trait our postmodern marketplace is dying to experience—it's up to us as godly women to lavish grace on our worlds.

And yet, just as with every virtuous character quality of the Christlike woman, grace will not be met with favor by everyone in the marketplace. In fact, those we encounter may not even know that it is grace they really long to experience.

If, as a journalist, I could place myself in the king of Persia's court, one aspect I'd report on would be how the other young women in the harem responded to graceful Esther. I fancy her as an outcast—set apart from the others. A "teacher's pet" of sorts, who was focused in her efforts to please those in authority over her rather than on being just another one of the gaggle of girls googling at themselves in the mirror.

Haven't we all been tempted to treat our competitors for a prize with contempt, jealousy or even their milder cousin, cattiness. Some of my most frustrating moments have been when a trusted friend (or my mom) has looked at me with disapproval and intoned a long, sad, "Meow," reminding me of the inappropriateness of my words or deeds toward a fellow woman. I'd be willing to bet that there were girls in

Xerxes' harem who responded to Esther with jealousy, contempt or cattiness.

To the secular world, Esther's brand of grace can often smack of all that is distasteful. Those of us who attempt to express grace may be treated as doormats—or worse, we may be trivialized and ignored. Again, the same is true of most aspects of biblical integrity.

To those in the world, we who seek to exude a godly brand of grace seem to be living life upside down. Our entire mind-set and way of life is diametrically opposed to theirs. Jesus told us to expect as much. He warned His followers that they would be misunderstood, as aliens in a foreign land. And so we are, even today.

True grace that plays out in kindness and gentleness is not weakness (as the world often believes), but it is strength. For example, when judgment (or valid criticism) is in our power and we choose to exercise the restraint of grace, we are exhibiting a more powerful strength than if we had taken the first opportunity to crush the one who is worthy of our anger.

Elizabeth, for several decades an administrator at a large city high school, describes the kind of grace God calls His daughters to exhibit as we assume positions of responsibility at work:

> In First Corinthians 16:13-14 we read, "Keep your eyes open for spiritual danger; stand true to the Lord . . . and whatever you do, do it with kindness and love" (TLB). Well, I try to put these things into practice every day. I try to be kind and caring to people. I would hope that—with caring and kindness and love—people would realize there is something dif-

ferent about me. Certain people know that I am a Christian. I wouldn't say my whole faculty knows, but I would hope that God's light shines through my actions.

Bestowing Favor in Love

What is grace, anyway? One simple biblical definition would be "unearned favor." In fact, throughout every dictionary definition of *grace*, the word *favor* keeps cropping up. As the *Nelson's Bible Dictionary* puts it, grace is "favor or kindness shown without regard to the worth or merit of the one who receives it and in spite of what that same person deserves." This is especially true of the grace of God which provided for our salvation. He paid the ultimate price for our sins, not because we had earned it and not because we were deserving. Instead, in His matchless grace, He loved us when we were unlovable. He lavished His grace upon us when justice would have required our eternal punishment.

This brand of grace freely offers a gift with no expectation of repayment. No debt is incurred by an act of grace; there is no obligation on the part of the recipient.

I experienced this kind of grace in a memorable way several years back, in a voice mail message from my boss's boss. I was on the road on a speaking tour, booked to give at least one speech per day (some days as many as three) on time management for the duration of the tour. I had been suffering on and off for two weeks with laryngitis (a debilitating illness for a speaker). Late in the day on Friday, this gracious man posted a message in my voice mailbox. He had no admonitions. No instructions. No additions to my workload. Not even a request

for a return phone call. Just a few words: "I care. I know you'll
do a great job. I'm praying for you." This message—and more
importantly the reminder that my friends and associates were
standing with me in prayer—strengthened my resolve and up-
lifted my spirit. That's grace, my friend.

Jenny, a respected pediatrician, describes a tangible evidence of grace that God has equipped her to exhibit in difficult and painful circumstances:

> I do a lot of work with abused children. Among
> the people who work with abused children are law
> enforcement officers, social services workers, district
> attorneys, defense attorneys, counselors, physicians.
> There's a delicate balance—not stepping on any-
> body's toes. I had to learn to not make my own turf
> be the most important thing in the world. If I do this,
> the child is the one who suffers.
>
> When you're dealing with hurting kids and hurt-
> ing parents, nobody cares who's the star—at that
> point they're looking for a person who is knowledge-
> able and authoritative, but who's a servant. Some-
> one who cares about them, while diagnosing their
> kid's disease.
>
> We have to learn to see the hurting person behind
> the belligerence. Respond to that person rather than
> react to the turf infringement. Some doctors get up-
> set every time somebody suggests they get a second
> opinion. But I'm a mom too. And if I didn't feel good
> about something, I'd want you to say, "Sure, get
> somebody else to look at this." So I try to treat my
> patients like I want to be treated myself.

Just as Jenny demonstrates, the truth remains: Grace is a
choice, an attitude that overflows from my heart and plays out

in my actions. When I'm standing on a train platform for twenty minutes—enduring below zero wind-chills with snow blowing across my face as engineers hook up a new engine—what kind of attitude will I portray to those huddling nearby? Will I grumble at the conductor? Will I make a scene because my right to an on-time train is being infringed upon? Or instead will I wait patiently, knowing the engineers are doing their job and that soon enough "this too shall pass"?

How about when I'm driving? Do I become impatient with the elderly driver in front of me who is driving ten miles per hour under the speed limit? Is that how I'd like my eighty-four-year-old grandmother (who still has a driver's license) treated by other drivers?

Grace does not come naturally to us.

The other day, my mom was backing her long sedan into a parking place. She was moving as quickly as she could on an icy lot. Next to her, a woman in a car was beeping her horn impatiently—obviously frustrated at the momentary delay. Suddenly, their eyes met. The impatient woman turned out to be my good friend's mother. Her impatience quickly turned to red-faced embarrassment as she recognized my mother.

Again, grace does not come naturally to us.

One way we can demonstrate grace in action is when we speak well of others. The logical end to this thought is that when we speak well of others, by implication we speak well of God. In this we hear echoes of Jesus' words: "When you did it to one of the least of these . . . you were doing it to me!" (Matthew 25:40, NLT). Christ's reputation before a watching world is enhanced when you and I act graciously, out of love for each other and for those in the world. Jesus told His disciples, "By this all men will know that you are my disciples, if you love one another" (John 13:35).

Just yesterday, I was the bearer of bad news to a client. Someone on his team was providing him with shoddy materials. I couldn't do the job for which he had hired me until this team member did his work. I worked to be gracious, not placing blame, only stating facts. But then my client asked me, directly: "You know the man. Why would he do this?"

My first inclination was to tell my client what I thought of the man and why I thought he was providing inadequate work. It would have been easy to vent—I might even have been justified. But it was as if I heard the voice of God prompting me to enhance this man's reputation, rather than to tear him down. Thankfully, I heeded God's voice and speculated only that the man might not understand the purpose of the project. The call ended with the client promising to discuss the matter with his worker. My relationship with both men remained intact because God gave me the strength to season the truth with grace.

The Siamese Twins: Grace and Truth

Have you ever stopped to think where truth would be without grace? Have you ever known someone who blurted out the truth without exercising the balancing virtue of grace? It is not a pleasant feeling to take the brunt of graceless truth.

So often we think of integrity as truthfulness and honesty. While these are a part of the mix, integrity is much more. Integrity calls for a lifestyle that is guided by an ethical code which in the Christian's case is laid out in detail in the Scriptures.

When the Apostle John set out to give readers of his Gospel their first glimpse of Jesus, his poetic description includes this oft-memorized statement: "The Word became flesh and made his dwelling among us. We have seen his glory, the glory of the One and Only, who came from the Father, full of grace and truth" (John 1:14). Did you catch that last line? Jesus Christ wasn't simply full of truth (although He *is* the perfect embodiment of truth; John 14:6), He was full of grace. I once heard a preacher say, "Grace without truth is permissive; but truth without grace is brash and distasteful."

I had never thought of it quite that way, but the preacher was correct.

Holly, whose story opened this chapter, in recent years served several terms as an elected member of her local school board. During her tenure, she was a key player in making difficult and unpopular decisions. At one point, Holly and her colleagues had no choice but to close down a popular ninety-year-old high school because of declining enrollment and cutbacks in government funding. Here's how she recalls the events:

> I remember a particularly angry public meeting when we had to vote to close the legendary high school. *What am I doing here?* I wondered as I watched members of the overflow crowd take turns at the microphone. For two hours they scolded us, threatened us with recall from office and criticized us for being unfeeling and out of touch. What hurt most was that I knew some of the people who spoke with such cruelty. I didn't object to them disagreeing with my views, but they so often accompanied their comments with personal attacks. For weeks the local

newspaper printed letters to the editor that targeted us—by name—and urged people to write and phone us. They did.

I've worked hard not to remember my critics' names, not to hold a grudge and not to save any of those newspaper clippings. What I *did* save—and will never throw away—is a stack of personal notes from people (some of them strangers) who reached out and offered me grace. Many of them didn't agree with my position, but they wrote, "thanks for being strong," "we respect you," "hang in there" and "don't take the criticism personally." I even got messages on my answering machine from people I barely knew who would say, "I know you have a difficult meeting tonight. I'll be praying for you."

What strikes me about Holly's story is that many of those who expressed grace to her did not agree with her decisions. They were truthful about the disagreement. But they expressed displeasure without the disgraceful cruelty others employed.

It is not only possible but also imperative to be both gracious and truthful. These two qualities are Siamese twins with a shared heart—neither is sufficient without the other.

Holly, who after many terms recently chose not to run for reelection to the school board, offers a useful perspective from someone who has felt the pressures of the political arena.

We often rush to judge our public officials on the basis of little information. We don't take time to learn the facts but react with emotion instead. My future role with our school system will be that of a support player. It's a role I will take seriously. I plan to offer encouragement and grace to whomever takes my place on the hot seat.

Dressed Up in Christ

One of my favorite New Testament passages describes our Savior.

> Have this attitude in yourselves which was also in
> Christ Jesus, who, although He existed in the
> form of God, did not regard equality with God a
> thing to be grasped, but emptied Himself, taking
> the form of a bond-servant, and being made in the
> likeness of men. (Philippians 2:5-7, NASB)

Now that's grace! Could it be that when we clothe ourselves in grace, we are—in some way—clothing ourselves in Christ?

Those who clothe themselves in Christlike grace come in many shapes and sizes. A school child may demonstrate grace by choosing an "uncoordinated" child for her kickball team because she doesn't want her playmate to feel left out. Or she may share her lunch with a child who doesn't have anything to eat, not expecting anything in return. These are the exceptions to the general rule of the school yard, because by nature humans are selfish—we take care of number one first. If there's anything left, then we might share and only then if others are watching. The child's selfless actions are grace. They don't come naturally. They are more than a "random act of kindness." They are intentional actions that come out of a heart that is filled with love and grace.

How many opportunities do we have to exhibit grace in the marketplace? When JoyAnn was working as a headhunter and trainer in a personnel placement organization, she had daily opportunities to show God's grace to people who were in dire straits. One woman came to her with few skills, but with a desperate need for a job. JoyAnn trained the woman in office protocol and found her a position as a receptionist. But the woman did not own a wardrobe appropriate for an office setting. So, JoyAnn went home to her own closet, gleaned a week's worth of professional skirts and blouses, and brought them to the woman. Because of JoyAnn's kind, caring attitude, the woman accepted the gift in the spirit in which it was offered. She didn't feel demeaned, but rather she responded positively to JoyAnn's genuine desire for her to succeed in her new job. And succeed she did, in large part due to JoyAnn's generosity and grace.

Cultivating a Grace-full Heart

If it's true that a graceful heart is contrary to our fallen natures, then how can we cultivate a heart that overflows with grace for the men and women with whom we come in contact? Let's look briefly at the example of a New Testament woman whose graceful, giving spirit won God's favor. The woman was Anna. She was aptly named, as *Anna* comes from the Hebrew word *Hánna*, meaning *grace*. Anna's story is told in only three verses of the Bible; she is mentioned only by the Gospel writer Luke. Yet she was a key player in the dedication of the infant Jesus.

> There was also a prophetess, Anna, the daughter of Phanuel, of the tribe of Asher. She was very old; she had lived with her husband seven years after her marriage, and then was a widow until she was eighty-four. She never left the temple but

> worshiped night and day, fasting and praying.
> Coming up to them at that very moment, she gave
> thanks to God and spoke about the child to all
> who were looking forward to the redemption of
> Jerusalem. (Luke 2:36-38)

Did you catch that sentence in the middle of the Scripture passage? Anna "worshiped night and day, fasting and praying." Anna learned grace from its source. She spent countless hours in God's presence. In his commentary on Anna's story, Matthew Henry notes, "She was a constant resident in or at least attendant in the temple. . . . [She] not only observed the hours of prayer, but prayed night and day; was always in a praying frame, lived a life of prayer."[1] In contrast to the religiosity of the Pharisees, Anna "not only did that which was good, but did it from a good principle, and with a good end; she served God, and aimed at his honour."[2] Because of her dedication, because of her heart's purposeful fixation on worshiping God, the Master favored Anna with the privilege of touching the infant Jesus and prophesying about the entrance of the Savior of the world—she had the opportunity to speak well of Christ before a watching crowd in the temple.

We've heard the old wives' tale that after years of marriage a husband and wife begin to look, sound and act like each other. To some degree, this holds true. As with every aspect of life, we become most like the one with whom we spend our time. Anna spent her time serving God, conversing with Him, no matter what other mode of service she was involved in. In so doing, she became more and more like God—in speech and actions. And she soon came to exude His grace.

The same will hold true for us. We needn't necessarily become twenty-four-hour-a-day residents of a church building, but we can become permanent fixtures in God's holy throne room, even as we go about our daily tasks in the workaday world. "Pray continually" (1 Thessalonians 5:17), the Apostle Paul wrote to first-century Christians. And the words hold true today. Pray always—no matter what external task we may be undertaking—pray that our conversation and our actions will consistently balance truth and grace.

We also would do well to remember that one of the evidences of grace—one of the ways it plays out in our lives—is when we speak well of others. We can beware so that our words and actions speak well of our Lord in the hearing of a contrary world.

In that context, think about what an awesome opportunity Anna received. She spoke well of Christ to all who would listen in the Jerusalem marketplace. There's no higher call for a graceful, godly woman than to speak well of Christ—whether in the marketplace of Anna's day or in our own postmodern culture.

Questions for Prayerful Consideration

1. When have I been tempted to blurt out the truth without tempering it with grace?
2. When others respond negatively to me, when they misunderstand my motives and misinterpret my actions, how can I temper my responses with grace?

3. How does the vitality of my prayer life enhance the character quality of grace in my everyday interactions at work and at home?

4. What specific steps can I take to demonstrate the character quality of grace in my workplace? In my home? In my committee(s), club(s) or church work?

5. How can I be a good example of graceful living that my children or my fellow believers in Christ will want to emulate?

Endnotes

1. Matthew Henry, *Matthew Henry's Commentary on the Whole Bible*, New Modern Edition Electronic Database. "Luke 2:25-40" (Copyright 1991 by Hendrickson Publishers, Inc.), p. 25.

2. Ibid.

Proven Trustworthy

Like the coolness of snow at harvest time
is a trustworthy messenger to those who send him;
he refreshes the spirit of his masters." (Proverbs 25:13)

Bev's Story: University Administrator Measures Her Words

I can remember having to tell someone that she wasn't going to stay in her job, that she was going to be let go. Over time, I had developed a good relationship with this person. She didn't work directly for me, but she worked for someone who worked for me. I knew he was not an easy person to work with, but I didn't want to end-run him, either. It was he who asked me if I'd talk to her; I decided it would be best if I did.

On many other occasions I had demonstrated that she could trust me and that I was honest with her. So when I sat down with her, I just laid out for her how I saw the situation. We discussed for some time her various strengths. I was straightforward with her, clearly saying, "This position is going to end for you," but I didn't stop there. I told her, "What we need to think about now is how you can make the best of this situation. Let's talk about how we can do this in a way that is positive for you."

It wasn't an easy thing to do. But in a way she was actually grateful in the end. I think her sense of trust in me, that I wasn't just feeding her a sugary line but that she could believe what I was saying, helped her come away with the assurance that she was going to survive and that she did have some good qualities.

It's easy to throw around compliments that don't carry much meaning. I try to be careful about that, so that if the time comes when what I say about someone in a positive way or a negative way really matters, they have already learned that they can trust me.

*H*ow often do we find ourselves saying: "You can trust me when I tell you . . ." or "To tell you the truth . . . " or "Really, I mean it . . ."

Why do you think these have become staples in our twenty-first-century vocabulary? I suggest to you that with a few exceptions (such as the example you've just read), truth and trustworthiness are in such scant supply in our postmodern world that when we are being truthful, we need to emphasize it, preface it with an exclamation, proclaim it from the mountaintops. We need to set our words apart as worth believing, against the cultural backdrop of communication that is deceptive and tricky.

Early in my childhood, my parents taught me that if I always told the truth, they would know they could always trust me. But if I lied, even once, they would never know whether they could believe me again.

Luke records Jesus' strong words to His disciples that sound remarkably similar to those I recall from my parents all those years ago: "Whoever can be trusted with very little can also be trusted with much, and whoever is dishonest with very little will also be dishonest with much. So if you have not been trustworthy in handling worldly wealth, who will trust you with true riches?" (Luke 16:10-11). In other words, the person who is dishonest in one area of her life is disqualified from trustworthiness in all other areas. In Jesus' eyes there is no compartmentalizing, no room for us to divide the spheres in which we cannot be trusted from the spheres in which we can.

Trust is a concept a tiny tot can grasp and yet in some ways it seems too difficult for our sophisticated culture to recognize. We can all name dozens of leaders (politicians, supervisors, employees, even churchgoers) who think that their professional and personal ethics are unrelated. As women of faith, we must be careful not to pattern ourselves after these leaders, who speak and act more often from deceitful, self-serving motives than from truth. I, for one, want my words and promises to be so unquestioned that they need not be proven and verified before they can be accepted.

Yet the temptation is great for every one of us to withhold some element of truth from our accounts of a situation, to slant a story to make ourselves look better, to add a little helping of exaggeration to an otherwise truthful word. Why? Because lying and dishonesty and shifting of blame are as old as the serpent's temptation of Adam and Eve in the Garden of Eden. They have become as natural to us as breathing and as unnoticeable as the flicker rate of our computer monitors.

So then, are we slaves to dishonesty? Or is there some way for us to consistently speak and act truthfully?

What's So Great about Trust?

Listen to corporate executive Ann's description of the role trustworthiness plays in her workplace persona:

If I make a mistake—it's horrible. I hate making mistakes. I get pale. But I admit the mistake openly. It's better to have it out there and get rid of it. So number one, I don't lie to my coworkers. Number two, they trust me because I would never try to make a name for myself by diminishing them.

I'm not saying this because I want to pat myself on the back, but because I have an overdeveloped conscience. I need to sleep nights. And there are some things I couldn't do and live with myself. It wouldn't sit well.

Also, I'm known for being a good soldier. Even though I don't always agree with a corporate decision—I'm certainly not talking about something that's unethical, but in the case of a decision I don't think is the best choice—even then I do my job. And I do it as best I can. I don't try to sandbag it so I can say, "I told you so."

Call it what you want: faithfulness, stability, constancy, "staying true," reliability, steadfastness, dedication. Trustworthiness is a character trait we can cultivate—with God's help. And if we are seeking God's pleasure, it is a trait we *must* exhibit consistently. Why consistently? Because trust is fragile and is easily undermined. As a crystal flower vase with a hairline crack is useless because water leaks out, so is trust that is marred by even one breach.

Why must we cultivate trust? It is one of the most basic building blocks of civilization. Every institution in our civilization is built on some element of trust. Our monetary system is backed by the trust, the "full faith and credit" of our government. Our marriages rise and fall on whether mates maintain faithful, true-to-their-word relationships with each other. We board planes, trains and automobiles trusting them to be in good repair; trusting the pilots, engineers and drivers to be equal to the task of transporting us safely. In the workplace, we all have at least a small element of trust in our employers: We trust that if we put in our forty (or fifty or sixty) hours, our employers will pay us our agreed-upon wage.

One dictionary defines trust as, "Firm reliance on the integrity, ability, or character of a person or thing" and truth as, "Sincerity, integrity . . . freedom from deceit or distortion of fact."[1] Any definition of trust contains an element of truthfulness. Their root is the same. We cannot trust without truth; only pure, unadulterated truth earns our trust.

Mercifully, trustworthiness is a character trait God exhibits in abundance. Says the psalmist, "The statutes of the LORD are trustworthy" (Psalm 19:7); says the ancient Hebrew king, David, "O Sovereign LORD, you are God! Your words are trustworthy" (2 Samuel 7:28). No matter what degree of trust we can (or can't) place in those around us, we can always trust God to be and do what He says.

So, when He promises, "Come to me, all you who are weary and burdened, and I will give you rest" (Matthew 11:28), I know He's not shading the truth; He's not making a one-time-only offer with fifty lines of fine print for me to wade through; He's not masking a hidden agenda; He's not going to sneer in my face and cackle, "I lied through My teeth." The fact of God's faithfulness to His Word—that I can fully and always depend on Him to remain a provider of good gifts—is the security that allows me to nurture an at peace inner spirit even when the phone is ringing, the staff is chaffing, the boss is demanding and the client is complaining.

Bringing this concept back to her workplace, Ann points out: "People know I don't lie. You would think that can't be all that different than the rest of the corporate culture. But indeed lying is all too prevalent. Yet every one of my bosses has always said they could depend on me never, ever to lie to them."

I challenge you to open your Bible and take a glance across almost any page of the Gospels. Note how often Jesus, when speaking to the multitudes or to His little group of followers, begins a discourse with the word "truly." (Also translated into English as "verily," "assuredly" or "I tell you the truth.") Clearly Jesus was speaking to people who were not always able to determine whether they could trust the speaker (sound familiar?). And He was using every opportunity to demonstrate that in contrast to human speakers, He is always true to His word and His words are always true.

And so, the greatest reason for cultivating trustworthiness in our own lives is rooted in the fact that it is a trait our God values highly—not just for Himself, but for each of us.

In First Timothy 3, Paul specifically calls on women of faith to be "temperate and trustworthy in everything" (3:11). Elsewhere in that passage Paul mentions other traits of the godly person. He specifically refers to deacons, saying they ought to be "worthy of respect, sincere . . . not pursuing dishonest gain" (3:8). Although the verse relates to a specific role within the church, the principles of godliness cited there can be applied to all of the faithful. These all boil down to the concept that the believer must be honest and truthful in order to be entrusted with leadership.

Think for a moment about the great liberator of the Israelites, Moses, who became overwhelmed with the work of leading and judging the multitude of people on their desert-journey to the promised land. Seeing Moses' weariness, his father-in-law Jethro made the following suggestion, "But select capable men from all the people—men who fear God, trustworthy men who hate dishonest gain—and appoint them as officials over thousands, hundreds, fifties and tens" (Exodus 18:21). For now, we'll gloss over the wisdom of the principle of delegation which Jethro shared with his son-in-law. Let's consider, for a moment, that in his counsel, Jethro equates the trait of trustworthiness with honesty, assuming it is a necessary by-product of fearing God. In fact, trustworthiness marks its bearer as one who fears God. Only this brand of honesty qualifies one for leadership in God's kingdom.

Similarly, in His parable of the talents, Jesus tells of a master who entrusts three servants with a portion of his property while he is away on a long journey. When the master returns, he asks the servants to give account for the way they invested his property. To the two who invested wisely, using the property to multiply the wealth, the master says, "You have been faithful with a few things; I will put you in charge of many things" (Matthew 25:21). Clearly, our master God is calling us to faithfulness or trustworthiness in those areas He has entrusted to us—only then can He trust us with greater things.

The Downside of Trustworthiness

But before we jump on the trust-mobile with both feet, let's count the cost.

In other chapters we'll spend more time examining the solutions modern-day women are applying to daily issues of character. However, as the concept of trustworthiness is foundational to integrity, let's concentrate primarily on the original source—on examples described in the story of God's people.

Sometimes our choices, in themselves, carry an element of danger. Consider the decision Queen Esther faced. When Mordecai explained the Jews' plight to her, the queen demonstrated for us a great lesson about counting the cost. She was not quick to promise that she'd handle everything. She understood the consequences of raising the king's ire—her predecessor, Queen Vashti, had been Exhibit A in Consequences 101. And so Esther did not give her word lightly, but she weighed the costs against the potential benefits. However, once she gave her word, she not only devised a solid plan to risk her own life and position to save her people, but she also followed the plan through—to the letter.

Sometimes the cost flows out of the jealousy and deceit of those around us. The Old Testament tells the story of the godly prophet Daniel. If you've ever wanted to see someone who maintained his commitment to godly truth and integrity in the face of tremendous difficulty, Daniel is the perfect example. Although he and his nation were captives, slaves of King Darius the Mede, Daniel's character took him places. Listen to this account:

> Now Daniel so distinguished himself among the administrators and the satraps by his exceptional qualities that the king planned to set him over the whole

kingdom. At this, the administrators and the satraps tried to find grounds for charges against Daniel in his conduct of government affairs, but they were unable to do so. They could find no corruption in him, because he was trustworthy and neither corrupt nor negligent. Finally these men said, "We will never find any basis for charges against this man Daniel unless it has something to do with the law of his God." (Daniel 6:3-5)

I'd recommend reading the rest of the story. But here are the highlights. The administrators convince King Darius to make praying to God illegal. Daniel is caught praying despite the new law and he is tossed into a den of hungry lions. You'll recall that the God in whom Daniel trusted shut the mouths of the lions and delivered him from certain death (6:22).

But I'd rather we focus not on the eventual outcome, but on the fact of Daniel's distinguished character and his unswerving faith in God before he knew the outcome of his actions.

The king recognized that Daniel was unquestionably trustworthy. Because of this, Darius was about to promote Daniel, making him second in command of the kingdom. (Daniel was one of three administrators; the satraps were the administrators' subordinates.) Not only was Daniel of good character, but even the pointed scrutiny of the jealous colleagues could not uncover a hint of corruption in his work or in his life. Daniel showed them up for their self-serving motives, their corruption, their negligence to fulfill all of the duties of their positions. Rather than determining to conduct themselves in the same way to bring credit and justice to the entire government, these men instead chose to focus their efforts on entrapping Daniel.

Likewise, as we work to distinguish ourselves as trustworthy employees and managers, some around us will be pleased, while others may work to bring about our downfall. Jealousy will do that. So will guilt. Sadly, it's to be expected—even in our Christian endeavors.

How does all this apply to our lives today? What consequences might we encounter if we choose to make trust a priority in our careers? Eyes wide open, we must make our choice, counting the cost. Maybe it won't put our mortal lives in jeopardy, but pursuing impeccable character could have a substantial cost in our career advancement.

Bev, whose story we heard at the beginning of the chapter, is a senior administrator of a major university. She says she earned the trust of her superiors and subordinates over the course of many small, seemingly insignificant interactions. "Early on, I didn't do some things that would have been self-serving, making myself highly visible." In other words, she chose to elevate others over herself, to give subordinates credit for their good accomplishments and ideas and to allow her superiors to take the limelight when she could have demanded her fair share.

These early decisions did not allow her to move as quickly through the organization as she might otherwise have done; others were promoted ahead of her. This seemed detrimental and discouraging. Yet she says, "I tried to live by my Christian ideals and character because principles matter a lot to me."

Having seen Bev's workplace conduct firsthand over a period of many months, I can attest to the fact that although she is more private about her faith than some, her actions and character choices bring credit to the God she serves.

Will we, like Bev, choose to pursue character, developing the trait of absolute trustworthiness? Is it worth the risk? Let's go back to post-lions'-den Daniel—untarnished, untainted with spite or revenge.

> At the first light of dawn, the king got up and hurried to the lions' den. When he came near the den, he called to Daniel in an anguished voice, "Daniel, servant of the living God, has your God, whom you serve continually, been able to rescue you from the lions?"
>
> Daniel answered, "O king, live forever! My God sent his angel, and he shut the mouths of the lions. They have not hurt me, because I was found innocent in his sight. Nor have I ever done any wrong before you, O king."
>
> The king was overjoyed and gave orders to lift Daniel out of the den. And when Daniel was lifted from the den, no wound was found on him, because he had trusted in his God. (Daniel 6:19-23)

Building Trust

Bev recalls,

> After I came to a position of authority and had it for a while, others began to get a sense of how I operated. They knew I wouldn't be artificially nice to

them. I wouldn't throw around compliments that
didn't carry much meaning. They knew I would tell
them the truth. They knew that what I would say to
their face was what I'd say behind their back. They
knew I would give them fair and honest treatment.

In the end Bev was elevated to a position of authority over
hundreds of highly educated staff members, but first she
needed to earn the respect of her colleagues and the trust of
her superiors.

Bev also points out that trustworthiness has another
component: confidentiality. At the beginning of her career
she determined never to betray a trust and to maintain confidentiality as a sign of respect for her employer and her employees. She has not breached that trust, even in situations
when the choice has been difficult to sustain.

I have heard people fault Queen Esther for not being
up-front with the king from the beginning about her Jewish
roots, saying she wasn't completely honest, that she might even
have been misrepresenting herself. But I have learned not to be
so quick to judge another's motives. As I read the text, I am
more inclined to believe that she was maintaining a trust—the
trust of her cousin Mordecai—when she kept her nationality a
secret. In Esther 2:10 we read of this strong admonition, "Esther had not revealed her nationality and family background,
because Mordecai had forbidden her to do so." Esther, like
Bev, knew how to keep a secret and maintain a trust.

For me, confidentiality is the most difficult aspect of
trustworthiness. My style is to be open and honest. I'll never
master the art of the poker face. Anyone who knows me at
all is able to plainly read my feelings in my face.

One incident when confidentiality was particularly difficult for me was when our division was reorganizing. My staff
saw me rushing in and out of meetings. I was requesting
odd-sounding information from them about their time us-
age, their workspace requirements and more. I was sure
they knew something was up and yet I was not free to confide in any of them—even in my most trusted assistant.

Two things kept me from telling all: my prior commitment
to maintaining the trust of my superiors and the knowledge
that the in-limbo, back-and-forth discussions of management
would cloud my staff's thoughts and hinder their efficiency. I
was, however, more than a little relieved when the gag order
was lifted and I was able to explain to my team how the reorga-
nization was going to affect each of them.

Restoring Trust

But what if we've already broken a trust? What if we've
given our word and not followed through? What if we've
lavished compliments upon the undeserving only to find
that, when our words are crucial, they mean little to the
hearer?

Ask any spouse whose mate has been unfaithful whether
trust can be restored. The answer is likely to be "yes and no."
While Christ's blood is sufficient for our forgiveness and our
cleansing before God, and while He calls upon us to forgive
each other, there is a certain wisdom in understanding that a
person who habitually deceives will likely do so again. Justified
wariness becomes a barrier to a fully restored relationship.

What I have found, though, is that owning up to my fail-
ures willingly—before someone else has the opportunity to

catch me—goes a long way toward restoring faith. This is not the easy road, but it is the right road.

I run a public relations and writing business. One of the hazards of this business is the constant tyranny of deadlines. As I stated in the opening chapter, I pride myself on never promising what is not within my ability (or authority) to deliver and always delivering what I promise. But "never" is such a difficult standard to maintain.

On Monday, I promised a client that by Tuesday afternoon (yesterday) I would deliver a small project to her. So, early yesterday morning I sat at my computer to work through my to-do list, starting with writing this chapter; her project was number two on the list. But the telephone began ringing (all the way through to 10 p.m.), and I found myself answering phone inquiries and replying to e-mails instead of checking items off my list. (I was quite a bad example of the time management principles I teach in workshops across the country!) Time got away from me and I never once opened the file containing my client's project. Sheepishly, I've just had to zip an e-mail to her confessing my failure, apologizing for not keeping my word and setting a new date for delivery. I find myself wondering, though, whether she'll find it harder to count on my new promise because I failed to keep my original one. In her situation, I might find it difficult, and that grieves me.

Questions for Prayerful Consideration

1. Is trustworthiness a trait I not only value in others but also choose to live out consistently myself?

2. Are there circumstances in which I have broken a trust? How can I attempt to rectify those errors? How can I keep from breaking trust in the future?
3. What are some ways I can prove my trustworthiness to my employer? to others with whom I have working relationships?
4. As one who hopes to move to positions of greater responsibility, what will I begin to do now to build a foundation of faithfulness, trustworthiness and consistency?

Endnote

1. *American Heritage Dictionary*, Third Edition Version 3.6p, "Trust" and "Truth." (Copyright 1994 SoftKey International, Inc.)

Four

Unquestionably Loyal

Now, a person who is put in charge as a manager must be faithful. What about me? Have I been faithful? Well, it matters very little what you or anyone else thinks. I don't even trust my own judgment on this point. My conscience is clear, but that isn't what matters. It is the Lord himself who will examine me and decide. (1 Corinthians 4:2-4, NLT)

Christina's Story: Public Defender Faces Dramatic Ethical Dilemma

As a public defender, I was called upon to represent a man charged with a serious crime. All of the evidence the state's attorney had presented made it appear likely he was guilty. Yet the man maintained his innocence to me. He wanted to proceed to trial.

I won't tell you what my personal beliefs were, because I don't feel I can do that. I did a lot of soul searching, though. Could I do a good job for him in the event that my personal beliefs differed from the stance he was maintaining? I came to the conclusion that yes, I could do a good job for him because I really didn't—and still don't—know whether he was guilty or not.

Ultimately, he pled guilty. But my soul searching was valuable to me. I came to the conclusion that although the nature of what he was accused of was disturbing, if he had wanted to continue to pursue going to trial then that's what we would have done, and I would have done a good job for him. That's because I had accepted the responsibility of doing that job. If

I were unable to do that, I would have had to find someone else to represent him. If that were the case, then I probably shouldn't be doing that type of work.

In our criminal justice system, that man deserves a defense. Why? There will come some situation—and you read about these all the time—where someone innocent is jailed or put to death. The people who represent criminals, the people who sentence criminals, the people who investigate criminals or accused criminals, are all human. Mistakes do happen. Everything is subject to the circumstances under which they are perceived. People's own personal beliefs—whether an investigator is tired or a judge had a fight with his wife—all come into play when a judgment is being passed. Everyone deserves a defense.

The soul searching Christina describes from her experience as a public defender (now she's a family law attorney) came at a time when she was reevaluating her priorities. It was one of many scenes that helped crystallize for her the answer to the question of where her loyalties lie. "My priorities are my family, then my work. I think, though, that living the way you set your priorities is more difficult than setting them," she says. "A strong family life is my priority. I'm doing what I can to make sure I achieve that. If I feel at some point I'm not doing a good job in my employment, then I'll make the decision not to do that or to do something else that doesn't cost me my family life."[1]

Call it what you will: priority, allegiance, loyalty. It's a trait employers solicit (but do not always offer), spouses prize, employees appreciate in their managers and children crave from their parents. It is a trait in high demand and low supply in our fast-paced, if-you-won't-promote-me-I'll-find-someone-else-who-will culture.

In one generation we've moved from the work ethic symbolized by my own father's job history (he spent thirty-nine-and-a-half years working for the same employer, who promoted him through the ranks, paid for his training and offered a pension for his retirement), to a generation that is resigned to the fact that slight downturns in a company's fortunes (or mergers with competitors or conglomerates) may mean we have a valued job one day only to find ourselves out-placed the next.

Loyalty. The *American Heritage Dictionary* defines it as "steadfast allegiance or faithfulness to a person, ideal, cause or duty." It carries with it the concept of stability, determination, readiness to serve, willingness to submit our own rights to a cause greater than ourselves.

Yes, loyalty is a prized commodity. But it is also a costly one.

Each of us will come to a crossroads where the competing priorities of bosses and employees, customers and colleagues, work and home, husband and children, church and faith threaten to tear us apart. What we need at these times is a pecking order of sorts—a self-established, biblically based hierarchy that is predecided so it kicks in when external pressures overwhelm us.

A Life Well-Ordered

When I was heading up the development team for the *Believer's Life System Women's Edition* day planner for Moody Press, I

found myself an overnight expert on the subject of life ordering, or life management. I was engulfed in the principles of the
system: giving God the highest place of priority in our daily lives
through Bible study, devotions, prayer and church participation; giving our families a high priority in time and energies;
planning and setting goals for our work lives as well as our spiritual and family lives; keeping it all together using (of course) the
planning system we offered. These were, I discovered as I began speaking to groups across the country on the subject, principles I had been trying to live out in my own life as early as my
high school years—and as recently as the previous day.

As I looked into the eyes of women (and men, too) who had
paid to attend my workshops, I saw a deep longing for freedom
from the tyranny of the urgent. These people—especially the
women—needed someone to release them from the guilt that
society heaps onto those who find that balancing a career, a
house, a couple of children, a husband, a faith, a church life and
more leaves them tottering on the brink of certain destruction.
And so evolved a presentation I titled, "I Can't Say 'No' and
Other Time Management Myths." To this day this is one of my
most popular speeches because the issue just won't go away.
And the solutions, while simple, are elusive. Here are some of
the highlights from that talk, which many conferees have told
me they found quite doable when they returned to their daily
schedules.

Solution 1: Determine to find God's will before seeking my own.

Fundamental to every other principle, this solution involves seeking guidance through Bible reading and prayer on

a daily basis. It involves setting myself and my desires at the feet of the God I have chosen to spend my life serving. It involves saying as Jesus did on the night before His crucifixion: "Father God, here's what I want to happen. Here's why it seems best to Me. But I acknowledge that My perspective may be limited. You may have something altogether different in mind. So I want You to know that even if it conflicts with what I've just told You I want, I am determined to do Your will without as much as a second glance at My own" (author paraphrase, see Matthew 26:39, 42).

Solution 2: Set priorities that place God's will at the head of the line.

This means making time for that Bible reading and prayer on a daily basis. It also means setting aside some of the things—be they media viewing, reading materials, offensive music, whatever—that compete with God for the prime-time slot in our lives.

Solution 3: Detach myself from the guilt of trying to please everyone else.

How often have you said, "I just can't please _____ (fill in the person's name)." You're right. You can't. But here's the news flash: You don't have to. If each of us has a personal relationship with God through His Son Jesus, then that relationship is the one by which all other relationships are measured. And God who created us—who understands (because of Jesus' time on earth as a human being) what it's like to be constrained by limited energies, limited time and limited resources—is the

One who sets our agenda. He's the One who loves us and who tells us He will never set before us any task that He will not equip us to accomplish. This is one of the most guilt-breaking revelations you will ever have.

Solution 4: Begin to break tasks down into manageable bites.

Say to yourself, *This portion can be accomplished in ten minutes, this portion will need thirty minutes, I'll be able to complete this chapter by the end of the workday tomorrow,* etc. This solution seems mundane after the lofty theology of the previous solution but it is nonetheless essential to ordering our lives. Because once we have determined that God has called us to set a particular role high on our priority list, we determine to put all of our energies into completing that task. If we are to accomplish it, we must set up a plan of attack. This principle will help us do just that.

Solution 5: Make time to celebrate.

This is a biblical part of the process. God established numerous seasons in His people's calendar to throw big, boisterous, jubilant parties. Why? To celebrate is to rejoice in how far we've come. To celebrate is to thank God for equipping us and enabling us to move from what we were to what we are today. To celebrate is also to look forward to what is coming next, the new challenge, the new adventure, the new opportunity.

There is, of course, much more to the setting up of our life's priority system. But I hope these solutions turn out to be the impetus that challenges you to establish a newfound chain of loyalty in your life.

The Loyalty God Models for Us

Why, in a chapter that highlights the character quality of loyalty, have we begun our discussion with a lengthy trip into the world of priority setting? Because to live a life marked by loyalty we must begin with an examination of those people and tasks to which we owe our allegiance. Now that we are on our way to knowing the answer to that question, let's take the next few moments to examine the most telling, and most costly, example of loyalty that I've ever encountered.

No one is more loyal than the God we serve. He is loyal to His own character in that He is consistent, changeless, unaffected by circumstances. He is loyal to His word. When He promised the people of Israel His blessings if they would serve Him wholeheartedly and His curses when their loyalty strayed, He followed through on His promise on both counts—consistently, over the course of dozens of generations.

And God continues to be loyal to His people, to His church, to you and to me. He is committed to keeping His promises to us: that He would never leave us alone and without comfort, that He would grow us into flowering trees that bear bushels of fruit, that He would even now be preparing a place for us to live a glorious ever-after in His great kingdom.

But what of the reverse side? What have we as people given back to this loyal Creator? In the days of the Old Testament, true believers were often few and far between. By and large, the people were loyal to God when their leader was godly; but when the king or judge was corrupt, whole generations of Israelites turned away from serving the true God and built temples to foreign gods.

One element of disloyalty of God's people can be seen in the setting of the book of Esther. Reading back through the words God spoke through His prophets when He allowed the people to be carried off into exile because of their evil ways, we find His plainspoken promise (in Jeremiah 29:10-11) that after seventy years in exile, God would bring His people back to the Promised Land to fulfill His plans for them to give them hope, a future and eventually the promised Messiah, Jesus. The promise was fulfilled when the conquering Babylonian kingdom itself was conquered by the king of Medo-Persia. In the first year of his rule, Medo-Persian King Cyrus wrote this decree: "The LORD, the God of heaven, has given me all the kingdoms of the earth and he has appointed me to build a temple for him at Jerusalem in Judah. Anyone of his people among you—may the LORD his God be with him, and let him go up [to Jerusalem]" (2 Chronicles 36:23).

At the time of Esther and Mordecai, the seventy years had long been completed. Zerubbabel and his construction crew had already taken Cyrus up on his offer and returned to the Promised Land to rebuild God's temple.[2] But, for whatever reason, an entire population of Jews still existed in cities throughout Xerxes' kingdom.

Even though these Jews had not returned to the land of Israel as they could have (and perhaps should have) done, God did not abandon them. Knowing that Haman would one day plot the destruction of all Jews in the kingdom, God worked behind the scenes (not even calling attention to Himself by name throughout the entire account) to orchestrate the complex chain of events that gave the young Jewish woman Esther influence, position and access to the powerful Xerxes. This picture of God's loyalty to His people, even when they were not living according to His command, sets for us the marvelous example of loyalty that is bestowed, whether or not the object of that loyalty is deemed truly deserving.

A Loyalty That Seeks the Best

What does this loyalty, this allegiance, look like for human beings? Let's look at two scenes from the book of Esther for some good examples.

In Esther 2:21-22, we read:

> During the time Mordecai was sitting at the king's gate [listening for word about how his cousin Esther was faring in the king's household], Bigthana and Teresh, two of the king's officers who guarded the doorway, became angry and conspired to assassinate King Xerxes. But Mordecai found out about the plot and told Queen Esther, who in turn reported it to the king, giving credit to Mordecai.

We'll talk about giving credit where it is due in chapter 6 when we examine our credibility and our good name. But now let's turn our attention to two of the king's most loyal subjects: his beloved queen, Esther, and her secret relation, Mordecai. Recall the words God spoke through His prophet, Jeremiah, to the remnant of Israelites who were being carried off into Babylonian captivity: "Also, seek the peace and prosperity of the city to which I have carried you into exile. Pray to the LORD for it, because if it prospers, you too will prosper" (Jeremiah 29:7).

Mordecai and Esther lived out this admonition by seeking the best for Xerxes, by foiling the plot of the two disloyal guards and by bringing it to the attention of the king. They could have considered Xerxes an oppressor. His country had, after all, conquered the country that had deposited their people in this foreign land. Instead, as loyal subjects they did good for the one holding power over their lives.

Note, however, that when loyalty to Persian authorities would have required Mordecai to compromise his loyalty to the God of his fathers (by bowing down to Haman and thus breaking a commandment of God), Mordecai—like Daniel before him—had his loyalties in the right order. God first, before allegiances to earthly authorities.

The second scene I'd like to examine has Esther as its main character. It bespeaks a family loyalty, of sorts—a loyalty to her upbringing, her Jewish roots, her beloved cousin and surrogate father. A loyalty that was challenged by the customs of life as a member of the Persian king's court.

Esther, as you've probably known since childhood Sunday school days, although she was queen, could not enter the king's presence if he hadn't first called for her. And yet, when she learned through word from her faithful servants that Mordecai was in mourning, and all the Jews with him, over the plot of Haman to kill every Jew—legally, with the approval of her husband the king—she prepared herself (through three days of fasting and presumably prayer), dressed in her finest clothing, gathered up her courage and presented herself before the king.

Under normal circumstances, she would not have presumed upon her husband. She would have waited to be bidden.

And yet these were not normal circumstances. She had heard Mordecai's words, "Who knows but that you have come to royal position for such a time as this?" (Esther 4:14). So she acted out of allegiance—allegiance to the family who raised her and to the culture of her heritage, all of which called upon her to take this presumptuous step of faith.

What we see in Esther's example is exactly what Christina struggled with at the beginning of this chapter. It is a measured loyalty—a loyalty that submits to preestablished priorities, that allows the subject to remain true to her godly convictions. It is not a blind loyalty. After evaluating the situation, Esther, knowing what she must do, spoke the words that have since been immortalized, "If I perish, I perish" (4:16). She went into the situation with her eyes wide open, knowing the potentially dire consequences of her actions. Yet she approached the king anyway because she knew where her priorities lay.

Order in the Office

Now let's make one more shift on this topic, bringing ourselves to the most practical, nuts-and-bolts brand of loyalty that brings order and stability into our twenty-first-century work lives.

I'd like you to meet Carla, a modern-day woman of loyalty. Carla began her career in retail sales and proved herself so loyal that the family-owned company where she was first employed during high school promoted her to manager. After nine years in retail management with that company, she received a call from a former staff member (a fellow Christian named Nan), who recommended her for a position as a customs broker, clearing freight into the United States for large corporations. Just a few years into her career in this high-pressure field, Carla was again promoted to management. She continues to demonstrate her loyalty to her employers not just in length of service, but more importantly, in the way she represents her company to customers.

> I try to be friendly, interested in the clients I work with. I come in at the crack of dawn to get things done for customers, to meet their deadlines. If they call and say they need something delivered the next day, I will go home late just to get the job done. My fellow workers may think I'm crazy, that I don't have a life [as I write, Carla is preparing for her wedding next weekend]. But I'm being paid to do a job. Whether I am a supervisor on salary or being paid hourly wages, I take my job seriously. Would I only give half of what I can do for Christ? I don't think so. Why, then, should it be any different for my employer? I firmly believe that I'm not working just for my boss. In a very real way, I'm working for Christ.

Carla doesn't do a lot of talking about her faith. Instead, she works hard at living out her God-centered principles and lets her actions speak for themselves. She tells of a situation that occurred early in her career in customs clearance:

> Nan and I had a big client—this was a prestigious, national account for our company. Although it was our client, our manager cleared some freight through customs. Unfortunately, this freight was not supposed to be cleared. Because of this error, the client was going to pull its entire business from our company. It would mean a big loss of revenue, with severe consequences to our terminal.

My boss had to fly to meet the client, to beg and plead for us to keep the account. Nan and I took our lunch hour to go off together to pray that God would give our boss and colleagues the right things to say and the wisdom to save the account. I believe it was our duty to pray for our boss and to pray for the client, that God would soften their hearts.

Incidentally, that account is still thriving today. But the good outcome notwithstanding, Carla and Nan's example of loyalty is a quiet witness of just how we as believers truly ought to conduct ourselves in the workplace.

As Carla told me this story, I recalled words the Apostle Paul wrote to young Timothy, whom he was mentoring:

> I urge, then, first of all, that requests, prayers, intercession and thanksgiving be made for everyone—for kings and all those in authority, that we may live peaceful and quiet lives in all godliness and holiness. This is good, and pleases God our Savior, who wants all men to be saved and to come to a knowledge of the truth. (1 Timothy 2:1-4)

Carla's story reminds us that praying for those in authority over us (government officials, of course, but also our company, clients and bosses) is one of the best ways we can demonstrate our loyalty. She also reminds us that all of our prayers will come to naught if we don't live out that loyalty by putting our best efforts into the work we do every day, in every circumstance.

Questions for Prayerful Consideration

1. What are the areas in my life—the relationships, organizations and tasks—to which I owe my loyalty?

2. When these areas come into conflict, what is the hierarchy of my loyalty?

3. How does God's example of loyalty to His people encourage my heart and challenge me to be more like Him?

4. What is one specific way I can be more intentional in demonstrating my loyalty to my boss? my coworkers? my staff members? my family? my church? my friends? my God?

Endnotes

1. Between the writing of this chapter and its publication, Christina (now expecting her second child) resigned from her law practice to dedicate this season of her life to her husband and children.

2. According to the "History of Israel" timeline in *The International Inductive Study Bible*, King Cyrus decreed that any Israelite who chose to might return to Jerusalem to rebuild God's temple in the year 538 B.C. Zerubbabel and his work crew returned to Jerusalem in 536 B.C., and the temple was completed in 516 B.C. Esther became Queen of Persia in 478 B.C., a fully sixty years after the people of God were allowed to return to the Promised Land.

Careful Listener

Dear brothers and sisters, be quick to listen, slow to speak,
and slow to get angry. (James 1:19, NLT)

Rene's Story: Nurse Listens for a Different Heartbeat

My take on being a nurse is that every other person's life is more important than mine at the moment that I am caring for him. The patient is far more in need than I am. One key element to being a nurse is that I have to be a good listener, because often patients don't even know how to convey their needs. A patient can say one thing when he is really trying to say something completely different.

For example, I had a patient who had a complication after heart surgery. It was a minor complication, but it delayed his discharge from the hospital by several days. It wasn't anything bad or life-threatening, it was just something that had to be monitored. And he kept complaining and asking why this had to happen to him. I could see an anxiety and a need just by looking in his eyes.

So I said to him, "What I'm sensing is that you are anxious to get home. Is there something pressing in your life that you need to be home to finish?" He said yes. So I followed up by asking, "Is there a friend who can help you get done what you need to get done by the deadline?"

He said, "Yes. Maybe I should make that phone call." He made the phone call, got his business taken care of and we never heard another complaint from him about remaining in the hospital. It wasn't the fact that we had to monitor him for several days that was at the heart of his worry; it was something else behind it that he needed to be home to handle. Through being a good listener and hearing what he was trying to say, I was able to get to the heart of the matter. After all, his life, his illness and his recovery were the most important things at that moment.

*a*s a critical care nurse in the coronary care unit, Rene is not being melodramatic when she points out that attentive listening is a life-and-death issue during her workday. She says, "We nurses develop a sixth sense, an intuition, about a situation. We listen to our patients' words; we heed their body language; we listen with our eyes. Sometimes you can actually see what they are trying to say. It's the look in their eyes: Whether it's fear, happiness, uncertainty or apprehension, you can always pick up something by using all your senses. Listening, of course, is one of the major ones."

Listening is not any less imperative for those of us who are in other professions. How can we nurture that attentiveness to the needs and desires of the people we encounter every day? Rene, who before becoming the mother of two toddlers was a nursing educator at a teaching hospital, offers this tip: "I think just by having constant awareness of the people around you, understanding their personalities—how they function, their basic needs, their wants—by being perceptive, everyone can develop intuition."

Rene is right to remind us that perception or attentiveness is crucial to our success in the workplace. Listening involves direct eye contact. It requires a focus on the speaker that does not allow our eyes to wander to and fro across a crowd, looking for someone more interesting (or more important) with whom we'd rather be carrying on a conversation. Listening involves a body language on our part that says—nonverbally—to the speaker: "You matter to me. So I'm focused on what you're saying."

Why is focus so important?

Have you ever stopped to consider the number of cues our brains process moment by moment? From subtle and not-so-subtle sounds to every detail our eyes pick up to the things we touch and smell and taste and feel? Not to mention our own thoughts and emotions. Our brains process quite an odd assortment of data. If we're paying attention, if we're focused, we can sort through these cues to develop what Rene calls *intuition*, or what my news-reporter colleagues call *getting to the heart of a story*. Whatever you call the trait, it is a handy tool that, when sharpened, can enhance our effectiveness at work and at home.

Checking Our "Read"

A practical example of good listening comes from makeup artist Lori, whom we met in chapter 1.

> A client may come in and say, "I am a stay-at-home mom with three kids. I have five minutes a day for myself. What can you do for me?" Someone whose focus is only "sell, sell, sell," will say, "OK. Here's your a.m. regimen and your p.m. regimen. You're going to use six products in the morning and six at night, eye shadows, lip liner, lipstick, lip gloss . . ." That artist obviously wasn't listening to the client. So the client will

feel overwhelmed, dissatisfied, as if she is only being seen as a dollar sign. She won't come back.

By being a good listener, on the other hand, I might look at her reflection in the mirror and repeat back to her, "OK, Mrs. Jones. You have only five minutes. Let me show you an easy, quick regimen." That means everything.

Lori's scenario reminds us to use one of the key active listening techniques: She demonstrates to her clients that she is paying attention to what they are saying by rephrasing and repeating the gist of what she is hearing. In this way, she can clarify that she is, indeed, receiving the intended message before she travels too far down the customer service road. In so doing, she is checking her read of a situation to keep from going too far astray—rather than chancing misunderstanding a client and failing to meet her needs. As an added benefit, the client will feel better understood and better served because she has participated in the process of identifying her own needs and then seeing them met.

Even a Queen Needs to Listen

Let's turn our attention to the way this brand of attentiveness comes to play a paramount role in the life of Queen Esther.

Even before she became queen of Persia, Esther was a practiced listener. When she was preparing for her first encounter with the king, she asked the king's eunuch, Hegai, to advise her on what she should bring with her. Not only did she ask, but she also listened for the answer, acted upon the wise counsel and ultimately pleased the king.

Once she became queen, though, Esther was not finished listening. She did not suddenly turn into an insensitive, demanding, spoiled woman. She did not stop caring about her cousin Mordecai who had raised her. In fact, she trusted her servants to carry reports of Mordecai's welfare to her since she was required to stay inside the palace and he was allowed only as far as the gate.

It was through listening to Mordecai's caution about the guards' plot to assassinate her husband that Esther was able to get that life-saving warning to the king. And it was through listening to Mordecai's plea for help that Esther was able to shine forth in her finest hour, the hour for which God had destined her to become a part of the king's court.

Here's an abbreviated version of the account we read in Esther 4. "Esther's maids and eunuchs came and told her" that Mordecai was sitting at the gate attired in sackcloth and ashes—a sign of mourning in that culture (4:4). Esther responded by experiencing "great distress." She tried to cheer him up by sending clean clothes. When that didn't work, she "summoned Hathach, one of the king's eunuchs assigned to attend her, and ordered him to find out what was troubling Mordecai and why" (4:5).

Mordecai told Hathach all about the plot to kill the Jews and begged him to tell the queen to go to the king and plead for the lives of her people. Hathach reported back to the queen, and again she listened. But in her listening, she also wisely perceived the danger to herself of approaching the king without being summoned, to which Mordecai responded that her life was already in danger because she was a Jew.

Then Esther sent this reply to Mordecai: "Go, gather together all the Jews who are in Susa, and fast for me. Do not eat or drink for three days, night or day. I and my maids will fast as you do. When this is done, I will go to the king, even though it is against the law. And if I perish, I perish."

So Mordecai went away and carried out all of Esther's instructions. (4:15-17)

Do you get a feel for all of the listening and speaking going on here? We will talk more about the communicating (or talking) side of listening in chapter 10, but for now let's focus on the receivers of information. Who is listening in these scenes? Mordecai, certainly, and Queen Esther, but also Hathach and the queen's maids, who are her messengers, faithfully carrying her messages to Mordecai and his to her.

If Esther had not taken the time to listen to the initial report of Mordecai's odd behavior, if she had been too busy—or too unavailable, or had felt she was too important—to listen to news mere servants brought to her, she would have missed the opportunity for greatness that awaited her. If Esther had listened but had not been willing to take action she would have been destroyed in the process. (Mordecai's warning rings with prophetic truth: "For if you remain silent at this time, relief and deliverance for the Jews will arise from another place, but you and your father's family will perish" [4:14].) But instead Esther got it just right. She put into operation the perfect blend of listening, speaking, planning, praying and finally action.

In this scene from Esther's momentous life, we see in operation the entire process of listening. It is not a one-sided exchange. Instead, one person listens as the other speaks, then the second speaks while the first listens. This is conversation. Such give-and-take conversation is sadly lacking in today's workplace. Everyone wants to be heard but few take the time to actually listen.

Listening Has Its Own Rewards

Corporate meeting planner Jean adds this nugget of biblical truth to our growing body of knowledge on the subject of listening: "I keep the text of this verse in the planner I have open on my desk every day. It is Proverbs 1:5: 'Let the wise listen and add to their learning, and let the discerning get guidance.' It reminds me that when I am a good listener, I can learn a great deal."

I like the juxtaposition of the concepts of wisdom and listening in this proverb. "Let the wise listen," the writer declares. In other words, if we want to grow in wisdom, one good way to do that is to pay attention to what's going on around us. What are others saying? What aren't they saying?

Incidentally, as I am learning to trust someone at work (or at church or even in a social relationship) I listen closely to what he or she says about other people. Does he speak well of others? Does he tear others down?

I can still recall a blind date I agreed to a number of years ago. The friend-of-a-friend showed up at my home on time and proceeded to take me out to a nice dinner. But during conversation in the car, he began talking about our mutual acquaintances. It didn't take him more than a few moments to begin verbally taking down each person—as if each one were a bowling pin and his ball of words were hurtling toward a head-on assault down the center of the lane.

As I listened, I felt rather sick inside. I knew that even as he was tearing down others, he would at one time or another tear me down. I chalked it up to another failed blind date. It cost me only an evening, but whenever I think of that evening, I am reminded of how much we can learn when we listen with tuned-in ears of wisdom.

Listening and Speaking/Speaking and Listening

Similarly, Elizabeth, a school administrator whom you will meet in depth in the next chapter, quotes this memorable proverb written by the New Testament Apostle James, "It is best to listen much, speak little, and not become angry" (James 1:19, TLB). She says she reminds herself of this principle often as she is managing her staff.

> I have learned to see what happened first before I say anything. To let the parties speak. This is difficult when you have people who have had an altercation and they come to you angry. But it takes some of the flame out of it when you let them talk and get it all out of their system. Then I go back and reiterate, 'This is what I hear you saying.' That calms them down."

Rene, too, points out that listening has hefty payoffs in times of interpersonal dissension. "Often in the health care field there are power struggles between physicians and nurses. But by taking the time to listen—to understand someone else's

perspective on a certain issue—it becomes easier to render patient care. That helps the overall outcome for a patient."

As in Rene's nursing venue, Jean's weekday calling involves a healthy dose of listening. But unlike Rene, Jean often finds herself depending solely on what her ears pick up,
since much of her interaction with clients is by telephone.
She doesn't have the benefit of body language to assess
whether the client is satisfied, whether he is paying attention
when she is speaking or whether his words express exactly
and completely what he means to say. This situation can
make the task of listening more of a burden. Formerly a
travel agent with a full plate of corporate and individual customers, Jean recalls,

> I can't always get everything I need in just one
> phone call. I have to listen to the client—often over
> the course of several phone calls—because clients
> don't always tell us everything they want during the
> first call. Most frustrating, though, is that often, just
> when I have all the arrangements made, the client
> will call back and say, "I have to change my itinerary
> because I have a problem with this." Then they will
> go into telling me the whole problem—complete
> with all of the details. I listen to it all and do my best
> to make the changes that are necessary. But it is
> draining to be the listener—a whole day of it can re-
> ally get tiring.

Just as Jean must play the role of listener in her work, her
clients, too, need to sharpen their listening skills as they entrust her with their travel plans. She gives this typical-day
example:

Clients will call in to make travel arrangements for a meeting. They will have been given parameters by their companies—when they should arrive, where they should stay, when they should return. Often the client will want to deviate from the prescribed itinerary. I listen to the directives the company sets up ahead of time, and I listen to the special needs of each traveler.

They also need to listen to me when I give them flight options and when I ask them questions.

A few days ago we sent out a mailing for a group of 1,100 people, all of whom are traveling this Sunday. [Today is Wednesday.] Now, I know for a fact that the other agents and I always ask each caller to verify current address and phone number. Nevertheless, in the last three days I've had dozens of phone calls from people in this group who have moved and who therefore didn't receive the itineraries and other necessary information because the packages have yet to catch up with them at their new addresses.

Because these individuals weren't listening to our questions, we had to scramble to put together replacement packages for each of them and send them via FedEx.

I think we can all appreciate the frustration Jean and her fellow workers felt in that situation. And we can easily recognize from this example the fact that how (or whether) we listen affects our credibility, our reputation and our character in the workplace. We've all been there. Someone else's error or lack of planning or lack of attention suddenly creates an emergency in our offices, causing us to scramble or redo a task that we had done right the first time. When I endure a situation like Jean's (and it happens more often than I'd like), I am less likely to trust that client's information the next time we interact—that client's lack of listening plants a barrier in the middle of our relationship.

At such times, it helps me to return to a concept we've already covered: grace. I'm not always good at extending grace—although I am pretty quick to request it on my own behalf. But the appropriate response for me, for Jean—for each of us who encounters a faulty listener in the workplace—is to extend even more grace, to express the patience and kindness that Nurse Rene offered to her impatient patient in the story that opened our discussion on listening. After all, the only real solution for dealing with a faulty listener is to offer an even more attentive listening ear.

Listening with Purpose

The best example that I have encountered of a good listener comes from the pages of the New Testament—and it was a fellow woman, one whom Jesus commended for the priority she placed upon listening to Him. She sat at His feet as He taught, hanging on His every word. She set aside all of her other obligations (which, incidentally, infuriated her more practical older sister) so she could use her ears for the purpose for which they were created: to hear the voice of God, in this case of God the Son, Jesus. Her name is Mary, the sister of Lazarus and Martha.

Although Mary appears several times in the Gospel accounts of Jesus' ministry, never once do we hear Jesus saying to her what He often said to the prominent members of the

Jewish leadership: "You have ears, don't you? So why aren't you hearing what I'm saying?" He didn't say it quite that way, of course, but that's the gist of the text: "He who has ears, let him hear" (Matthew 11:15).

He didn't have to say that to Mary because she was already listening. I, on the other hand, am more often like the task-oriented Martha, who ends up smarting a bit after Jesus' chiding. You may recall the scene, described in Luke 10:38-42:

> As Jesus and his disciples were on their way, he came to a village where a woman named Martha opened her home to him. She had a sister called Mary, who sat at the Lord's feet listening to what he said. But Martha was distracted by all the preparations that had to be made. She came to him and asked, "Lord, don't you care that my sister has left me to do the work by myself? Tell her to help me!"
>
> "Martha, Martha," the Lord answered, "you are worried and upset about many things, but only one thing is needed. Mary has chosen what is better, and it will not be taken away from her."

Ouch. Don't you feel Martha's pain? If you're Martha the worker, Martha the busy bee, Martha the woman who always finishes her task with style and expedience, Jesus' words really hurt. They hurt most because they are spoken out of love and because they are absolutely true.

As women we may be internally programmed to be the take-charge workers, the go-to people, the give-it-to-her-she-won't-fail-us right hand the boss depends on. But there is a time to work and a time to listen. Both are important. And sometimes the listening must take first place, even ahead of the doing.

Questions for Prayerful Consideration

1. Who are the people in my workplace who most need me to listen to them?
2. Typically, how have I responded to these people in the past?
3. How can I develop the traits of a perceptive, or intuitive, listener?
4. When I am tempted to work first and put off listening, how will I discipline myself to listen as a result of what I've learned about the importance of this trait?
5. In the vitally important relationship between God and myself, what practical steps will I take to become an active listener to Him every day?

Credible Witness

Let love and faithfulness never leave you;
bind them around your neck,
write them on the tablet of your heart.
Then you will win favor and a good name
in the sight of God and man. (Proverbs 3:3-4)

Elizabeth's Story: School Administrator Requires Wisdom of Solomon

To me, integrity in the workplace is doing the job you're hired for. I have seen many dedicated teachers in the classroom. They put in a lot of time and effort. It is certainly not for the pay, but rather because they have that personal integrity that makes them want to do a job that is excellent.

Then I have seen the other aspect: people in the classroom who didn't teach, who took the easy road, didn't bother to grade papers, didn't plan, had outside activities interfering during the workday, even some who were double-dipping— running a business from school.

There are some teachers you never hear a complaint about; other teachers have parents in every day complaining about something. And I hear a *lot* of complaints; they sort of filter up to me. They come in from counseling or discipline or from the social worker. We talk with the parents and the student. In a separate interview we talk with the teacher, asking the teacher to respond to the charges made. Then we try to figure out what's really going on.

How do I know who to believe if each party is telling a different story? Consistency is the key. Is it an isolated incident or do I have five parents complaining of the same issue? Does this happen every semester to the same teacher? Is this a parent who complains about everything or is this a parent who has never appealed to me before?

Adding all of these issues and observations together, I get a feel for what's going on, even if I'm not in the particular classroom. All of these things play into the credibility of the teachers and the parents and the students.

Credibility or reputation is a critical commodity to Elizabeth, a high school administrator in a major city school system. She began as an English teacher, earned her Ph.D. and became an administrator. Elizabeth has spent more than thirty years building a reputation among her peers, her superiors and her subordinates as someone who has the courage of her convictions—someone fair, trustworthy, responsible and caring.

How has she worked to cultivate this reputation? Among other things, she says, "I try to be kind and caring to people. And I feel it is important to have a work ethic that doesn't leave a job undone. Also, I stick up for my principles, but that doesn't mean I have to tear other people down. I try to build them up. We may disagree, but this is a civilized world and we need to try to be civil about our disagreements."

The academic world is not the only place where our reputation can make or break us. Just this morning, my mother and I were talking about the subject of credibility and reputation. Her career ran for ten years before I was born and resumed when I went to college. She was a secretary, an administrator and a recruiter/trainer/sales manager at various points during those years.

When she returned to the job market after her sixteen-year absence, she got her feet wet as a temporary secretary, a position that offered her the flexibility to care for my father (who was recovering from heart surgery) and to visit me periodically in Indiana, where I was attending college and then graduate school. Mom's three-day assignments always turned into six- to twelve- to eighteen-month stints in a corporation. Why? Because by the time one department's work was complete, another department would have heard of her strong work ethic and would find a place to use her services.

Later, when she was employed as a recruiter at a new temporary office services franchise, she made sales calls on many of her former clients. Because she was known for her hard work, the clients were willing to give her new company a try. She received countless job orders in her new position simply because she was proven faithful in her previous encounters with those companies.

What's the Big Deal about My Reputation?

Among colleagues and superiors, Tammy (a news reporter whose story we'll hear more about in chapter 12) carries the name of one who does not undercut others to the boss, never steals projects or ideas to pass them off as her own and always completes assignments thoroughly and on time. I worked with Tammy several years back, and I can vouch for the fact that she is vigilant about, in her words, "dealing honestly and fairly with newsmakers and other information sources, as well as giving the public the most thorough and accurate reports possible."

But Tammy does periodically encounter others in her profession who are not so intent on maintaining integrity and honor:

> I've always been aware that in addition to producing for my employer, my credibility is always on the line with the public. One of the most trying experiences I had was when I was covering the municipal government of a small town and the editor's newsroom pet covered the county government. Being the newsroom pet unfortunately did not make him a good reporter, and it soon became clear that he was reporting erroneous information—when he managed to report anything at all.
>
> The problem for me was that our areas of coverage tended to overlap, and I kept getting calls—and pleas—from my own sources to set the record straight. So I did, which caused great resentment on the part of the other reporter—and the boss. It nearly cost me my job.

For Tammy, a good name before the public was more important to her than even her own boss's perception of her. And when it came right down to it, she was willing to put herself in hot water with the boss just to be sure truth was reported under her byline to the newspaper's readers.

And yet, as will be the case for us in certain circumstances, the world—or the boss, or our colleagues—may misinterpret our intentions and tarnish our good name, as Tammy's boss did when she corrected her colleague's blatant errors. In those times, the words of the Apostle Peter will ring as truly for us today as they did to their original readers two millennia ago:

> Be happy if you are insulted for being a Christian, for then the glorious Spirit of God will come upon you. If you suffer, however, it must not be for murder, stealing, making trouble, or prying into other people's affairs. But it is no shame to suffer for being a Christian. Praise God for the privilege of being called by his wonderful name!"
> (1 Peter 4:14-16, NLT)

Tammy's lifelong concern for building a credible reputation and a good name did pay off in other more long-range circumstances, if not at that moment in that particular newsroom. She recalls, "I've rarely ever had to apply for a job. I've been recruited for most of them based on my performance in prior positions. I was specifically recruited for at least one that I know of both to bring professionalism to the office and to enhance the company's reputation in the community."

Consistency Is at the Heart of Reputation

Even outside our own homes and our own companies our reputations will precede us. When I was promoting one of my books, I stopped at a newly opened Christian bookstore in the same town where I teach college English. When I approached the owner and introduced myself, she said, "Oh, *you're* Julie Ieron. I understand you teach English at the Bible college. I've heard about you—you're tough but fair." Where did this bookstore manager hear about my reputation? Unbeknownst to me, one of my students had taken a part-time job in that store. So my name as an author was to be linked with my conduct as an instructor—connecting two venues I would normally have assumed were virtually unrelated.

Now, the reputation of "tough but fair" is one I can live with. In fact, I rather like it. It expresses how I want to be thought of by the students whom I challenge toward excellence each semester. But the scene in the bookstore was a great reminder to be careful about how I conduct myself in every situation—I truly never know who is listening or who I will encounter again at a crucial juncture.

What is one of the world's favorite criticisms of Christians? I'm sure you've heard it. I know I would be quite wealthy if I had a dollar for every time I heard the indictment that Christians are hypocrites, saying one thing and doing the opposite.

I believe we can combat this indictment only if we work every day, and in every setting of our lives, to maintain consistency between what we say and what we do. If we say we are hard working, or if we demand hard work out of others, then we must be willing and consistent in the standard of hard work to which we hold ourselves. Similarly, if we claim to be true to our word, we should never be caught in a lie. If we offer a listening ear, we should never be caught gossiping or dispensing privileged, confidential information without permission. It's all a matter of creating harmony between what we claim to be and who we really are.

Ye Olde Grapevine

Even when we are working hard at establishing our reputation at work, there is at least one aspect of our reputation over which we have little or no control. Unfortunately, there is an Orwellian organism that is alive and well in every organization and it can be one of the biggest contributors to our reputations. What is it? The office grapevine. Believe me, it is pervasive—and quick. Few members of any team are beyond the influence of the grapevine. It is the proverbial *they*. (As in, *they* say, *they* aren't ever wrong, etc.) It never fails that somehow, before you know what's happening in your own life, *they* know all about it.

Let me show you what I mean. After spending several years as a senior editor at *Moody* Magazine, I was invited to apply for a promotion to become managing editor of Moody Press, another division of Moody Bible Institute. Both the magazine and the press were located in the same building but on different floors. Since I was unsure whether I wanted the promotion, I didn't mention it to anyone other than my own boss. (It was his boss who asked me to pursue the job.)

However, one of the more astute members of the press staff perked up her antennae when she saw me walk downstairs for a lunch meeting with the editorial director of the press. Before the promotion was officially offered or I had taken time to consider the opportunity and determine whether I would accept the job (in fact, before that first lunch meeting was even over), she had already surmised that I would be her new boss. I didn't even have the opportunity to make my own first impression on my new staff (I did accept the job); ye olde grapevine did it for me.

According to veteran administrator Elizabeth, that was a fairly typical occurrence. She offers this counsel: "No matter where you work, there is a grapevine that brings forward some of the credentials you have. Such as, 'She's easy to work with,' or 'She's a real bear,' or 'She doesn't know what she's doing.' You can't always control whether the information is good or bad or where they got it, but they will have an impression of you, a preconception."

Elizabeth says one good way to counteract such preconceptions is that as we "begin to work with people, try to show them direction and support. Over a period of time, try to help them understand that all you're asking from them is for them to do their job. You're not demanding; you're making them a part of the team and asking them to join in and contribute to the group." In this way, she says, we will be able to build on the best parts of our reputations and dispel those bits of grapevine gossip that may be untrue, unproductive or unflattering.

Known for Their Good Name

As I was considering biblical examples of women who live out the principle of maintaining a good name or reputation in the public arena, my mind went immediately to a seldommentioned Old Testament name: Huldah. Now you're probably saying, "Who? Never heard of her."

Bear with me. Huldah is an obscure woman who had a profound impact upon my life. So much so, that when I was invited to record a three-minute TV segment highlighting the life of one Bible woman, of the fifty-two profiled in *Names of Women of the Bible*, I chose to highlight Huldah. After poring over her story, here's what I wrote about this woman of influence and reputation in a king's court:

Huldah's husband served as keeper of the wardrobe in King Josiah's royal court. But it was she who was well-known in the court for her gift of prophecy. Obviously, God in His providence planted her in that place at that time. She was a contemporary of Jeremiah and Zephaniah. Yet for some reason when King Josiah sent messengers to inquire of the Lord, God led them to Huldah, who lived a few buildings away from the royal palace.[1]

Bible commentator Matthew Henry explains: "they had had more and longer acquaintance with her and greater assurances of her commission than of any other; they had, it is likely, consulted her upon other occasions, and had found that the word of God in her mouth was truth."[2] I concluded my observations of Huldah by noting that she "had proven trustworthy over a lifetime of ministry. . . . She spoke the word of the Lord with courage and conviction."[3]

Why did this prophetess affect me so powerfully? Because as far as I can tell Huldah toiled every day in obscurity. She lived a regular life. She was a wife, probably a mother. Yet she was also called by God to speak His words. By maintaining an example of godliness, she established for herself a name that became well-known because of her consistently accurate words from God, even during a time when her fellow citizens didn't act as if they knew God or cared what He would say to them.

I like Huldah because her world looks remarkably similar to the world you and I live in. It is a world where God and His ways are foreign, ignored, trivialized. Yet there will be

moments—maybe even just one moment in a lifetime—
when God puts in our path genuine seekers, as He put good
King Josiah in Huldah's path. In those times He gives us His
words to speak with conviction and courage. In the mean-
time, though, He calls us to live out a lifetime of daily
days—days of consistency, days of obscurity—remembering it is those days that build our credibility for moments of
defining greatness.

We see this principle at work in the life of Queen Esther
as well. In the last chapter Esther was on the verge of approaching the king unbidden—with not a little trepidation.
She was nonetheless resolute, certain that she was undertaking a necessary mission. Well, here's what happens next:

> On the third day Esther put on her royal robes
> and stood in the inner court of the palace, in front
> of the king's hall. The king was sitting on his royal
> throne in the hall, facing the entrance. When he
> saw Queen Esther standing in the court, he was
> pleased with her and held out to her the gold
> scepter that was in his hand. So Esther ap-
> proached and touched the tip of the scepter.
>
> Then the king asked, "What is it, Queen Es-
> ther? What is your request? Even up to half the
> kingdom, it will be given you." (Esther 5:1-3)

I am quite certain that it was God, working behind the
scenes yet again, who allowed the sight of Esther to please the
king. Nevertheless, it seems to me that the king must have
known this favored wife well enough to recognize that if she
had taken the ultimate risk of entering his presence unbidden,

it must be a matter of grave urgency. I mean, the man offered her half of his kingdom. That would not have been a trifling gift. But here again, this woman of character had a reputation that preceded her, a good name, a credible witness in the eyes of her husband, the king. Because of her good reputation, the king was of a mind to give her whatever she asked when she made a request.

Esther obviously did not go running to the king with every trivial detail of snubs and snipes that likely went on among the wives and concubines in the harem every day. (Imagine sharing your husband with all those other women. Or if that's too difficult a picture for you, just imagine *that* many women living in close proximity. Even if they weren't sharing a husband, all that togetherness and tedium would certainly foster an atmosphere of pettiness.)

I fancy that Esther was aware that a large part of credibility can be found in knowing when to smooth over a rough spot with grace and when to make an issue of something quite serious. It comes down to the concept of choosing our battles wisely, of not sweating the small stuff and instead saving our favors to call in when the matter is sufficiently weighty to warrant it.

Enhancing Christ's Reputation

Jenny, a kind and loving pediatrician who serves her state by examining and treating children who have been abused (we'll run into Jenny again in chapter 8) is troubled by the view we Christians often present to a watching world. Similarly troubling is the reputation we must live down among our unsaved peers and neighbors because of a few folks on the radical fringe who regularly make news. She points out,

> I think Christians are among the worst arguments for Christianity. Seriously. We bicker and we fight and we slander each other in front of other people. In so doing, we're slandering God's name—even taking it in vain.
>
> When we treat people arrogantly or we don't take time to listen to them, we do harm to the kingdom.
>
> Jesus said they'd know us because we love one another. If we aren't listening and we aren't showing that little bit of love—even to the people in the checkout at the grocery—if we don't treat other human beings respectfully, then we're not showing them how Jesus would treat them. It is so important that we don't take the name of the Lord in vain by the way we act.

The Scripture verse that began this chapter is actually another way of expressing what Jenny is saying: "Let love and faithfulness never leave you; bind them around your neck, write them on the tablet of your heart. Then you will win favor and a good name in the sight of God and man" (Proverbs 3:3-4).

I am particularly drawn to the idea of connecting my actions of love and faithfulness with the favor and good name I want to cultivate in the sight of God (my primary audience) and people (my secondary audience). I agree with Jenny when she says our respect for others will show them we value and love them. When we do this consistently, we will place another block upon the building of our good reputation. And not only *our* reputation, but also that of the God for whose kingdom we hold the office of ambassadors to an alien world.

Questions for
Prayerful Consideration

1. When others speak of me (at work, at church or at home), what do I want them to say? How is this different from what they might be saying, based upon my conduct until today?

2. What are at least three steps I can take each day to be sure I am being the Christlike person I want to be in the eyes of those watching me?

3. What impact does my daily conduct have upon the way people view God and His kingdom?   ·

4. What specific things can I begin to do with regularity that will enhance Christ's reputation at my office? in my community? in my church? in my home?

Endnotes

1. Julie-Allyson Ieron, *Names of Women of the Bible* (Chicago, IL: Moody Press, 1998), pp. 26-27.

2. "2 Kings 22:11-20," *Matthew Henry's Commentary on the Whole Bible: New Modern Edition Database* © 1991, 1994 by Hendrickson Publishers, Inc.

3. Ieron, pp. 26-27.

Seven

Friend Worth Cultivating

Two are better than one,
because they have a good return for their work:
If one falls down,
his friend can help him up.
But pity the man who falls
and has no one to help him up! (Ecclesiastes 4:9-10)

Joan's Story: Accountant's Lifelong Friend Is Right on the Money

You ask about developing an inner circle of people we can trust, who will not betray a confidence. Well, that's very hard. Ronald Reagan said, "It's lonely at the top." As president of my own company, I found that to be true. You have to be careful—even about talking with pastors—because even they tend to talk to other people. When my mother was alive, she was a source of friendship for me. But once she and Dad were gone I had to do a lot on my own. I guess I pretty much relied on my kids [now adults] and some long-time staff members, but it was difficult.

I don't have a big circle of friends I can trust. But I do have Shirley. We attend church together, and we have been close over the years. She does some accounting work but she isn't one of my work colleagues. Shirley is someone I can depend on.

About a year ago, I experienced life-threatening health problems. At 10 p.m. on January 6, after writing my annual report, I was preparing for bed when I was hit with the most excruciating abdominal pains. I realized that I had better dial 911. It was near midnight when they took me to the emergency room.

The hospital tried to connect me with my daughter in California. It took three tries. As she sped to the airport she called her brother and then she called my wonderful friend from church, Shirley. It was 3:45 a.m. in Chicago, but Shirley got up, dressed and rushed to the hospital.

I remember finding her there as I returned to the emergency room from one test or another. Shirley stayed at the hospital with me all day while the doctors huddled to try to find my problem. When my daughter arrived, she stayed with her.

I don't have a big circle of close friends. But God has gifted me with the wonderful friendship of Shirley.

Joan is a friend to her staffers, to her family members, to her clients. She listens to their problems, offers godly counsel and makes time to pay attention to the lives behind the numbers. "For my staff, for clients, many times I would be sitting there and a person would be telling me all about his problems. I would say, 'Lord, please tell me what to say on this one.'

"I didn't just take their numbers. Anybody can be a number cruncher. I took their problems. I spent an hour with them instead of fifteen minutes. I didn't build my business like other people do: get them turned around as fast as you can. Some of my staff would say, 'You're never going to get rich this way.' So I'd say, 'Then I'll never get rich.' "

Being friendly and having a friend are two very different things. Just ask any woman who holds a position of responsibility in the workplace.

Attorney Christina says, "Before I took this job, a supervisor told me, 'Don't trust anyone, ever, in this field.' I found this to be good counsel." She points to friendly relationships she built with attorneys who previously worked in the same practice as she did. "Now when I call them, I can tell there's an edge, a *tone* to their voices." They are restrained, distant, mistrustful, because rather than colleagues, they are now competitors or, worse, opponents in the courtroom.

University administrator Bev, who has 250 employees reporting to her, has encountered a similar difficulty in building relationships within the community of her university. She notes,

> There is such a natural tendency with people you like to say, "You're not going to believe this story." I am sure that every woman in every management situation finds the same thing. You want to be an interesting conversationalist, but you're always guarding a little bit. Sometimes we make the mistake of being a little too girlish. I hate to stereotype women, but women do enjoy friendship and conversation.
>
> That said, though, I always have my guard up. It is a little lonely. That is the hardest part of the job. I share things with my secretaries that I wouldn't be able to share with anybody outside my office, because I've learned to trust them and I know they can keep confidences. But it's not personal.
>
> I have some female deans reporting to me. Even to them I can't say, for instance, "You are not going to believe what those guys said today on senior staff; they said the most sexist thing." I guess I've learned to internalize that—I've learned to talk to myself. I

share some with my husband, but it doesn't mean anything to him because he doesn't know the people.

The one place you can build a trusted inner circle of friends is with colleagues in a similar environment but away from yours. You can tell them about the situation; you can share the experience. They don't know the people so it won't jeopardize any confidences, but they do understand the circumstances. I have colleagues around the country that I can do that with, but I can't do it here at the university.

Editor Jodi calls these people "outside-insiders." She says,

I tend to stay away from anyone in my inner circle being in my workplace. It becomes an issue of setting boundaries. I don't talk about conflict at work with coworkers. However, I do have a couple of people whom I have met through work who have a God-centered outlook. Alma [a former missionary and genuinely kind woman] is one of those people. It helps to have someone like Alma, who is an outside-insider, who knows enough about my work situation that she can give me quality advice.

Even Just One Friend

Like Joan, Bev has nurtured one special professional friendship that has been a source of encouragement and joy and strength over the years. She and her friend Barb were colleagues in their early years as professors. Barb has since moved on to launch a now-thriving consulting business in a nearby city, but she continues to be the one person Bev can depend on to listen, offer wise counsel and commiserate over the difficulties of university administration.

Although she misses the close daily contact with her friend, Bev says, "In some ways it's better that she's not on campus anymore. She's somebody that I can share some of the work situations with now, because she's not here. I don't have to deal with violating a trust. We don't have as much time together as we'd like, but we stay in touch by e-mail, and we try to have lunch together. Everybody needs that set of friends."

Yes, everybody does need friends who are able to offer wise, objective counsel and who are far enough disconnected from the situation that we can share details without gossiping. Yet they need to be well-informed enough to listen and confront us with the hard facts when we are in need of an attitude adjustment—or worse yet, to tell us when we are partially to blame for a difficult situation.

Someone Who Won't Betray a Confidence

A refrain that recurred with amazing frequency when I asked professional women about how they choose a trusted friend is: She has to be someone who will never betray a confidence. If I tell her something of a private nature she will not broadcast it across the office or the campus or the church.

This is of particular concern in the legal field. Christina says, "I can never discuss my cases with anyone, which makes it difficult. Unless I can sort it out in my own mind, it just festers. You don't want that to happen, so you learn to sort it out yourself."

When she needs someone to talk to about issues outside the profession—issues of being a good mom, a good wife, a good attorney—she says, "My only outlet is my husband." Then she adds, as an afterthought, "I do talk to a couple of friends about the struggles of working and maintaining a family." Her cautious, attorney nature creeps up as she describes the criteria she has for choosing those friends: "Do I want to confide in someone who has her own dysfunctional problems? No! Because I won't get a good solution if she has her own problems."

In the opening story, Joan mentioned that even some professional ministry workers cannot be trusted with matters of a confidential nature. While this can be true, her comment brought to mind a circumstance that occurred in my own life several years ago that led me to the opposite conclusion:

> In one of the most frightening scenes of my life to date (and I hope ever) I was accosted at the door of my office in the middle of the afternoon by three thugs with a gun. My two companions/friends fled, leaving me to face the gunmen alone. Fortunately, the three were content to steal my purse and slink away counting their haul, leaving me trembling and panic-stricken.
>
> My employer offered to send me to a counselor, insisting that I needed to talk to someone. But I didn't feel emotionally equipped to build a trusting relationship with a stranger at that moment, so I called my pastor, Chuck Anderson. He agreed to counsel me and to pray with me. He listened without heaping guilt on me for allowing myself to become a victim (as a few people had already done) and he followed up over time to be sure that I was healing emotionally, letting me know he was concerned and hadn't stopped praying for me. He's the only person outside my immediate family whom I told about the incident.

(Of course, a large percentage of the campus community where I worked knew about it through the office grapevine, but after the initial police and security report, I did not discuss the incident with anyone else.)

Not only did Pastor Chuck prove to be a good friend and a wise counselor, but he never told another person in the church that he had been counseling me, let alone why—not his secretary, not the chairman of the board, no one. His wife, Lauren, never told anyone, either. I know this because it was two years later before I was able to talk about the situation, and when I did open up to fellow-worshipers, they were noticeably shocked to hear about what I had endured.

Pastor Chuck and his wife are the kind of people who qualify as inner-circle friends in my book. The kind who keep a confidence. Who offer wise counsel. Who base that counsel upon scriptural principles and bathe it with a healthy dose of prayer.

Why Are Friends So Important?

A passage from Proverbs comes to mind that answers the question of the important weight our choice of friends bears in our lives. "Do not make friends with a hot-tempered man, do not associate with one easily angered, or you may learn his ways and get yourself ensnared" (Proverbs 22:24-25). It stands to reason, the wise author counsels, that those whose counsel we seek, those whose opinions we value, will shape the person we become. If we are bosom-buddies with someone who makes poor choices, who lets anger cloud good judgment, who flies into a rage over trivial infractions, we will become like that person—in the worst possible ways. Conversely, in Third John 11, the apostle writes, "Dear friend, do not imitate what is evil but what is good. Anyone who does what is good is from God. Anyone who does what is evil has not seen God."

Often during my upbringing in the church, I heard the Proverb quoted (always in King James English) that says, "there is a friend that sticketh closer than a brother" (Proverbs 18:24, KJV). I always had the vague notion that the friend to whom the author was referring was God Himself. But then I read the description offered by Bible commentator Matthew Henry and this Scripture took on a new meaning to me. For not only is God the friend who stays close to us when others abandon us, but we too can become to our friends that kind of faithful, trusted confidante. Listen to Henry's comments:

> Solomon here recommends friendship to us, and shows what we must do that we may contract and cultivate friendship; we must show ourselves friendly. Would we have friends and keep them, we must not only not affront them, or quarrel with them, but we must love them, and make it appear that we do so by all expressions that are endearing, by being free with them, pleasing to them, visiting them and bidding them welcome, and especially by doing all the good offices we can and serving them in every thing that lies in our power; that is showing ourselves friendly. . . . In our troubles we expect comfort and relief from our relations, but sometimes there is a friend, that is nothing akin to us, the bonds of whose esteem and love prove stronger than those of nature, and, when it comes to the trial, will do more

for us than a brother will. Christ is a friend to all believers that sticks closer than a brother; to him therefore let them show themselves friendly.[1]

It all boils down to knowing where to go for friends and choosing those friends wisely. For whomever we choose to let past the pleasantries and into our hearts' confidence will influence who we become—for good or for bad.

With wisdom beyond her twenty-something years, makeup artist Lori says, "It's not that I don't have any friends who are non-Christians. I do. But the ones I seek advice from are Christian friends. Why would I want advice from someone who isn't going to use the Bible, who isn't going to direct me to Christ? I want someone Christ is going to speak through. Someone who is going to pray for me, who is sincerely going to care."

Lori offers this candid example, straight out of her daily life: "I'm single. All my non-Christian friends are trying to set me up with people who aren't Christians. But my Christian friends who are married are saying, 'Lori, hold out for the right one, someone who is going to put Christ first.' "

In the workplace it is no different. Corporate executive Carrie recalls an occasion when she faced a difficult situation with one of her employees. The person was purposely sabotaging a project and creating difficulties at every turn.

It so happened that during this crisis I had occasion to visit with a family friend during a social outing. This friend was a retired senior executive from our church. I asked whether he had ever faced a similar situation. He had. And so after describing the problem, I listened attentively to his counsel—counsel gleaned from his many years of experience.

When I returned to the office, I applied his suggestions and they worked. I won't say the employee
suddenly became a model of compliance, but the
situation was diffused and I was able to maintain the
coherence of my department. My work team remained intact as did my sanity. I can't help but feel
God guided me to that Christ-fearing man for counsel at that particular moment.

The Counsel of a Trusted Advisor

When I ask you to name a Bible woman who modeled
friendship, I'd be willing to wager that you'd quickly come up
with the name of Ruth, the young pagan woman who became
the daughter-in-law of the God-fearing woman, Naomi. Certainly a study of the intertwined lives of these two women,
these two friends, would yield a bushel of advice on friendship.
I would challenge you to read prayerfully the book of the Bible
that bears Ruth's name, looking for ways that God would prick
your own heart on 1) how to be the kind of friend who will
challenge others toward godliness, as Naomi did for Ruth; 2)
how to be the kind of friend who will surrender her own rights
and privileges to serve the needs of her special friend, as Ruth
did for Naomi.

But for now I'd like for us to turn our attention toward
two other friendship situations in the Bible. Because as important as *being* a friend is, our subject here is knowing
where to look to *find* a friend worthy of our trust.

The first woman I'd like us to consider is the queen of
Sheba. We meet her in the parallel Bible passages of First
Kings 10 and Second Chronicles 9.

> When the queen of Sheba heard about the fame
> of Solomon and his relation to the name of the
> LORD, she came to test him with hard questions.
> Arriving at Jerusalem with a very great caravan—
> with camels carrying spices, large quantities of gold,
> and precious stones—she came to Solomon and
> talked with him about all that she had on her mind.
> Solomon answered all her questions; nothing was
> too hard for the king to explain to her. When the
> queen of Sheba saw all the wisdom of Solomon . . .
> [she said,] "Praise be to the LORD your God, who
> has delighted in you and placed you on the throne of
> Israel. Because of the LORD's eternal love for Israel,
> he has made you king, to maintain justice and righ-
> teousness."
>
> And she gave the king 120 talents of gold, large
> quantities of spices, and precious stones. Never
> again were so many spices brought in as those the
> queen of Sheba gave to King Solomon. (1 Kings
> 10:1-4, 9-10)

This queen, the sovereign of a region in Arabia, harbored a
lifetime of questions in her heart. She was obviously a thinker,
someone serious and thoughtful about ruling her people with
justice and righteousness. Not satisfied until she could find her
answers and unable to find them at home, the queen of Sheba
embarked on a journey to meet with the one whose reputation
for wisdom had reached as far as her country. Not having any
equals among contemporaries in her own land, she journeyed
long and paid with many riches to speak with the wise King

Solomon of Israel. She poured out to Solomon all of the questions she had been accumulating in her heart and he answered them all, satisfactorily and completely. This queen knew to find answers in a man who held the reputation as one who would draw from God's vast storehouse of wisdom.

The second woman whose friends I'd like for us to note is the queen we've been studying throughout this book, Esther. In Esther 4 we read of the maids and eunuchs who brought word to Esther about Mordecai's sorrow. Apparently those servants had won the trust of the queen. They seem to have had knowledge of Esther's connection with Mordecai (her cousin and surrogate father) for quite some time, and never to have shared that knowledge among their fellow servants. I surmise this because, until Esther revealed her nationality to the king (I'm getting ahead of the story here), no one knew she was a Jew—not the king, not Haman, not anyone. Esther wisely, and by God's grace, had surrounded herself with a "staff" of individuals who were loyal to her, who could be trusted with intimate and life-impacting messages, without fear of incriminating information leaking into the wrong hands.

Esther didn't have the luxury of loading up a caravan and riding off to God's country to find wisdom, prayer warriors or answers to her difficult dilemma. She couldn't pick up the phone or zap an e-mail to a lifelong friend asking for advice or input. And yet God provided for her a trustworthy cluster of people who would do her bidding without compromising her confidences.

And so, we return to modern life where we are searching for friends who will spur us on toward godliness, friends who will challenge us to become better managers, who will pray for us when we are beaten down, who will faithfully keep our secrets without compromise. These friends, as difficult to find as they are, come directly from God's hand. The best counsel may just be to ask the God who sticks closer to us than even a member of our earthly family to provide for each of us the dependable friends who will serve this role in our lives. In so doing, let's work to be that kind of friend in the lives of those God brings across our paths.

Questions for Prayerful Consideration

1. Who are the people in my life who have modeled the kind of professional friendship that is evidenced in the lives of Bev and Barb, Joan and Shirley?
2. What lessons in friendship can I learn from a study of the lives of Ruth and Naomi?
3. What are the heart questions—the workplace questions, the career questions—that I need a friend to help me sort out?
4. What are the character traits that I'm looking for in an inner-circle friend?
5. How will I seek to be the kind of friend to someone else that I'd have her be to me?

Endnote

1. *Matthew Henry's Commentary*, Electronic Edition, entry on Proverbs 18:24.

Eight

Sensitive to Others

Therefore I . . . beg you to lead a life worthy of your calling, for you have been called by God. Be humble and gentle. Be patient with each other, making allowance for each other's faults because of your love. (Ephesians 4:1-2, NLT)

Jenny's Story: A Medical Doctor Finds Her Heart

During my first year of residency I was assigned to look in on a patient named Linda. She was seventeen and had acute leukemia, which was, at that point, a death sentence. She was the queen, the darling of the floor. The chief resident looked at me through his bushy black eyebrows and scowled and said, "There had better be no mistakes on this one."

Linda wasn't that much younger than I was. Soon she and I became friends. We would sit and chat in the evenings when my work was done. As it became apparent she was not going to survive her battle with leukemia, she began wanting to talk about her dying. One day in December, she said to me, "I don't mind dying so much. It's just that I'm seventeen and I've never done anything with my life; my life hasn't counted for anything."

We prayed about that together. And then God dropped an idea into my mind. That night I went to the fabric store and bought some fabric panels that could be cut, sewn and stuffed to make them into little dolls and animal toys. I brought them to Linda along with my sewing machine, and I told her, "I have an aunt who is a missionary in Colombia.

You make these up, and we'll ask my aunt to give these to children in Colombia. When she gives them away, she'll tell the children about Jesus. Some of them will come to Jesus, and in this way you'll be a missionary."

In the last few weeks of Linda's life, I kept popping into her room. Every time I did, she and her mom would be cutting and snipping and making those little dolls as if they were working on a trousseau. She got them finished and we sent them to Colombia just days before she died.

Last summer (nearly twenty years later), my aunt was back in Colombia, and she met two of the little girls she had given the dolls to. Now they are grown women, loving the Lord and working for Him. That's Linda's legacy.

This was an instance when God showed me that when you make yourself available to care for a person and not just to treat his or her low white blood cell counts, then He picks that up and He honors it.

*L*ooking back on her relationship with Linda, Jenny says, "You learn as a doctor to distance yourself to some extent, but you can carry that too far. There's a fine line between caring so much that you become unable to give the proper medical help and becoming just a technician, not a physician. A physician is one who cares for the whole person, not just the body. I hope to be a physician, not just a technician."

Being a true physician has its own costs, as Jenny quickly recalls. When her friend Linda succumbed to the leukemia, Jenny cried.

You grieve like anybody else does. One of the things I used to say to Linda is, "I'm so glad you know the Lord. Because when you leave, we don't say good-bye, just *shalom*—good-bye with the surety that I'll see you again."

When you care about those you treat, you become acquainted with grief like Jesus was. He was "a man of sorrows, and acquainted with grief" (Isaiah 53:3, KJV). I've often cried with patients. Instead of them perceiving my tears as coming from a position of weakness, I think they see it as a priceless gift. I've joined them as a mom or as a friend who's loved and lost rather than just as a technician who is finished with her job.

Critical care nurse Rene has a job that, as we already discovered in chapter 5, takes her right into the thick of the suffering of patients and their loved ones. "You might think that we'd get used to dealing with death and serious illness. But I am never resigned to the fact that this is just another day in nursing. I can remember every person who has died in my care, maybe not by name, but I can see his face and remember what it was that I dealt with at the time. I reconcile my feelings in thinking I am doing God's work, and it is my calling."

That's fine for Jenny and Rene and the medical profession—they can expect to deal with life and death issues every day. There isn't one of us who doesn't hope and pray for a sensitive doctor and a kind nurse to serve us in our times of illness or grieving. But what about those of us in other professions? How can we cultivate a sensitive, caring heart for those with whom we work every day and yet find the balance point that allows our professionalism to shine through as well? In this chapter we will spend a significant amount of time answering that question.

However, before we address the "how," I believe we should spend a few moments answering the "why."

The Feminine Dilemma

It is my observation that (being careful not to stereotype men or women) the character trait of sensitivity is tied in with who we as women were made to be. The nurturing tendency is one we all share deep down, to some degree or another, because that's how we're wired, how God created us. This trait, in particular, is one significant way we can add a texture, a richness to our workplaces that would not be there if we were not there. It's not that men can't be sensitive or caring—many are. But the trait is more visible in most of us as women when we are operating out of the strength of who we are.

On the other end of the spectrum, however, are women who have been working long and hard trying to build careers in male-dominated industries. The temptation for these women is to become as much like a stereotypical man as they can. To be gruff. To be uncaring. To be brash and rude and even crude. To lack even the slightest degree of kindness and compassion. They have assumed these personas because they believe it is what their male counterparts expect, and because they believe that is what it will take for them to garner respect—to be taken seriously in the workplace.

I contend, however, that when we women go overboard in projecting masculine traits, we actually set ourselves up for the opposite response from our male coworkers. Here's a good example:

Recently I was describing the purpose of this book to a thirty-something male friend who works in the dot.com industry. He's very trendy, very cutting edge—a true Gen-Xer in his outlook on life. That's why I was surprised when his ears perked up as I explained that in this book I was going to examine the roles and conduct of women in the workplace. In fact, he expressed the idea that this might be a book men would be interested in as well.

I was shocked. Then he explained that he works for a female boss who has taken the overly masculine route and that her demeanor has him questioning his role as a man and how he expects a woman to conduct herself. He told me, "I've never encountered a man who is as foulmouthed or as hard-nosed as my female boss is. If she cares about any of her staff, she certainly doesn't show it. She probably did have to push her way into a male world, but I really think she has overcompensated—it's not at all becoming. It makes her difficult—downright scary—to work for. After seeing women like her in operation we men are having a hard time trying to figure out who *we're* supposed to be—what role we're supposed to play and what role women are supposed to play."

It helps, sometimes, to see ourselves in the eyes of the opposite sex. By looking at ourselves through their eyes we may see that instead of garnering the respect and honor of the men with whom we work, we can become so much like them (in the worst possible ways) that they dread every interaction with us. I don't know about you, but I don't want any colleague or employee to see me the way my friend sees his boss.

Caring for Others from 8 to 5

So, what does a feminine woman who is in charge look like? How does she operate in difficult situations? Well, for one thing she doesn't deny her feelings and emotions; instead she finds appropriate ways to express them and in so doing improves a situation or a working relationship.

Attorney Christina says she sees the difference between the sexes in operation plainly in her work.

> Most men are not emotionally attached; they don't care as much about the feelings and the ramifications of a [court] decision as a woman would. When I was in criminal defense work, it didn't hit as close to home, so it was easier to deal with my emotions. I was working with people who get in trouble [driving under the influence of alcohol, assaults, etc.], rather than families. I was better able to give them advice and not take what they would tell me emotionally.

After her stint as a public defender, Christina went to work in a law practice that handles divorces almost exclusively. Every day she encounters husbands and wives and children who are in situations that hit closer to home. They are more like she is, more like her husband, her son, her friends and social acquaintances. These are problems she has more trouble setting aside at the end of the day. "I cry. I cry a lot. It gets to me," she admits. It is those tears that make her a better attorney, because she genuinely cares about what happens to the families, to the individual spouses and especially to the children of divorce. People are important to her. Helping people in difficult circumstances is why she entered her profession. And the way she values the people she serves is apparent in all of her interactions—with clients in her office and even with opponents in the courtroom. Christina takes the time to let each individual know she values him or her.

Simple Kindness

What does sensitivity look like in an office or workplace setting? Certainly it is evident in the medical and legal professions, and it is particularly conspicuous when absent. But it is as necessary in every other venue. School administrator Elizabeth works hard at being sensitive and caring and genuinely kind to her colleagues and her subordinates.

> Sometimes it just means saying a good word and supporting their endeavors, like saying, "Wow, you put a lot of work into that," or "Your kids may not have won the game, but they played hard," or "I've seen you working with those kids and you're doing a good job with them." Supporting one another is so important. We all appreciate it when someone gives us a good word and notices what we are doing. When our colleagues compliment us, it raises our own self-esteem.

Dr. Jenny offers this clarifying thought:

> The oncologist in the hospital where I trained had a sign on his door that said, "To cure sometimes, to help often, to comfort always." I think we as people can do that. It is costly. It means stepping out of our shell enough to be hurt. But it also means enlarging our lives and being an instrument of healing in another way than just pills or potions. It's something anyone can do. Compassion is hard bought, but it makes us better people.

She puts this concept into practice as she deals with even the tiniest patients she encounters in her pediatric practice:

> When I look at each child, I see potential. This child has a specific calling; God has a plan for him or her.

> Too often we don't realize the person we're talking *in front of* may one day be the doctor who's taking care of us, or may one day be our president. It's so important that we treat each child respectfully. So, when I meet a new child, without thinking about it I drop down to one knee so his or her eyes are on the same level with mine.

The Tricky Balance Point

Just as we all have encountered women who have assumed male characteristics at work, so we likely have encountered women who have gone too far to the other end of the spectrum. These are women who care so much that they become handicapped in their ability to carry out their daily work and are so concerned with other people's needs that they cease to do the job for which they are hired.

My first experience on this tottering bridge came early in my management career, when my student worker needed to be held accountable for not showing up to work when she was scheduled to do so and for socializing (instead of working) when she did come to the office. She had been through surgery, and her recovery was not as smooth as it should have been. I tried to be sympathetic by offering her leeway and by doing some of her work myself. But as the days turned into weeks and even months, it became apparent that she was taking advantage of my sympathy. Eventually, my boss decided that I needed to discipline her—to lay down the law of expectations and challenge her to meet these or surrender her job. Grudgingly I confronted her, but I came away feeling used and disillusioned. And when I started a new job a few months later, I was less inclined to extend patience and compassion to my new secretary because the bitter taste of this experience was still fresh in my mind.

As I recall this frustrating situation and wonder how I could have stopped it from happening, I ask again: Does sensitivity require that we become doormats, so concerned about everyone else's feelings that we handicap ourselves or fail to meet the goals set for us by our superiors?

This is an issue corporate bean counter Ann faces on a daily basis. A colleague once told Ann that she is dispassionate about the job, something she says he meant as a compliment, because that's what it takes to do her job successfully. And yet, she is not dispassionate about *people*—that's where she draws the differentiating line:

> As a woman and as a Christian I try not to yell, not to lose my temper, not to threaten. I am sympathetic about genuine problems. I make a point to help, whether that help is me or whether it takes allocating another clerical person to the department. I want them to know we are in this together. However, tough decisions do need to be made. I'm not unsympathetic at a personal level, but I do have to do the right thing without being angry or vindictive. I'll help wherever I can, but if they won't let me help and they cannot do the job, I make sure they understand there will be accountability.

A Change of Perspective

Accountant Joan encounters a similar dilemma when she is pleading her clients' cases before even the most fearsome of IRS agents. She has found it helpful to change her own perspective. Rather than perceiving the agent as an adversary, she says, "I remember when I am negotiating with anyone that God loves the person sitting on the other side of the table just as He loves me. Many of those men sitting across the table can be difficult, but the choice is mine to remember that God loves that man. When I treat the person on the other side of a negotiation with that firmly in mind, it even helps resolve the situation."

Interestingly, the refrain coming from sensitive women across the gamut of professions is some variation of this thought: We value people over circumstances, over numbers and profits, over a long client list or even our own reputations.

As we glance at the life of Queen Esther, the woman who has formed the basis of our discussion on the character traits of women who succeed in the secular marketplace and who are successful in God's eyes, we see that she demonstrated compassion and sensitivity in abundance. She lacked any measure of self-serving in her motives. She was willing to put herself on the line when she perceived that people for whom she cared were hurting. And when the king offered her riches and power unmatched among women of her day, she did not claim them for herself. Instead she elevated others (namely her cousin Mordecai, as we will see in the end of the story) above herself.

The ultimate example of compassion that we find as we look into God's recorded Word is found in God's own heart. What amazing compassion He must have experienced that He would care so much about the miserable, helpless state of you and me in our humanness that He would send His one and only Son to be tortured and killed, to pay *our* debts with *His* life. That brand of sensitivity is unapproachable for us. And yet Jesus does invite us to follow His example, to become like Him in every area of life.

Directing Compassion to Those Most in Need

One follower of Christ who gave herself away in compassion and kindness is a woman named Tabitha (also known as Dorcas), whom we meet in the book of Acts. Listen to the account of this caring woman's life, found in Acts 9:36-42:

> In Joppa there was a disciple named Tabitha (which, when translated, is Dorcas), who was always doing good and helping the poor. About that time she became sick and died, and her body was washed and placed in an upstairs room. Lydda was near Joppa; so when the disciples heard that Peter was in Lydda, they sent two men to him and urged him, "Please come at once!"
>
> Peter went with them, and when he arrived he was taken upstairs to the room. All the widows stood around him, crying and showing him the robes and other clothing that Dorcas had made while she was still with them.
>
> Peter sent them all out of the room; then he got down on his knees and prayed. Turning toward the dead woman, he said, "Tabitha, get up." She opened her eyes, and seeing Peter she sat up. He took her by the hand and helped her to her feet. Then he called the believers and the widows and

> presented her to them alive. This became known all
> over Joppa, and many people believed in the Lord.

A couple of phrases in Tabitha's story speak to me. First, she is said to have been "always doing good." Second, "all the widows stood around [Peter], crying and showing him the robes and other clothing that Dorcas had made" for them. The good Tabitha did was practical, useful and appreciated by those she served and by the other disciples who observed her service (those who sent for Peter and begged him to come to Tabitha's funeral). Unlike the bossy woman my male friend described earlier in this chapter, Tabitha used her talents and skills to compassionately serve the most helpless members of society. In her kindness, she garnered the respect of all the people she encountered. Her testimony, in fact, drew "many people" to believe in the Lord.

A third phrase that jumps out at me is that Tabitha is labeled as "a disciple," a pupil of Jesus Christ. In the English translation it is the same label given to Peter, James, John and the rest of the original twelve disciples. However, in the Greek language, the word changes when referring to a woman, as opposed to a man. It means the same thing; it accomplishes the same purpose. But the word takes on a different form: *mathetes* refers to the male pupils; *mathetria* refers to female pupils like Tabitha. The accents, the emphasis of the words, fall on different syllables. Yes, in her doing good, Tabitha was following the example of her Teacher, just as the male disciples were doing. But she was doing it in a way that was uniquely feminine; her accent was on a different syllable than that of Peter or the others.

That subtle distinction is of the same variety that appears even today in the caring heart God has placed in each of us as women. *Why* should we operate out of compassion? Because it is our God-given nature to do so. *How* should we do this? By valuing people over power for ourselves; by respecting individuals we encounter rather than building empires on the backs of those we trample on along the way; by seeing others as worthy of dignity and heartfelt sacrifice, just as our Master did. And if along the way He entrusts us with power, authority and a valued reputation at work, we will be prepared to use those gifts to demonstrate to others the compassion and kindness of God Himself.

Questions for Prayerful Consideration

1. What difference has Jesus' compassion meant in my life?
2. What are three specific things I can do to develop my own heart of compassion for others?
3. Are there individuals I encounter at work who are crying out for my compassion?
4. What are some specific ways I can express sensitivity and kindness to these people?
5. Are any individuals to whom I have shown compassion taking advantage of my kindness? How will I rectify those situations while staying true to my God-given character?

Nine

Prudent Planner

We can make our plans, but the LORD determines our steps. . . . The LORD demands fairness in every business deal; he sets the standard. A king despises wrongdoing, for his rule depends on his justice. The king is pleased with righteous lips; he loves those who speak honestly. (Proverbs 16:9, 11-13, NLT)

Ann's Story: Number Cruncher Takes Command

A planning team is only as good as the individual members. The weak link shows up when you give assignments, spreading them out amongst group members and the tasks don't get done. That creates an unfair burden for the rest of the team. One project where the team approach was not working was in our region's Y2K compliance preparation.

The task originally was not mine; my boss had assigned it to someone else. When the person responsible was transferred, responsibility for planning and compliance of our region's team fell to me. I asked for all the files and realized nothing had been done—and we were within nine months of December 31.

We had a mix of people on the team: Some thought it was ridiculous; others thought it was life-threatening. Some wanted to spend a bazillion dollars preparing for every contingency; others didn't even want to do the bare basics.

I can't look at that as one of my most successful team-leading experiences, because I was forced into a management mode called command/control. It was a management method that was frowned upon in my organization, but it was necessary. I started putting out mandates: You have to report this at this point, you have to check this system right now and so on. Even then, people were ho-hum about it. So, my boss set up a conference call and said, "This directive is coming from my office. If things aren't done properly and on time, heads will roll." Funny thing: Everyone complied from then on.

Later, we had a division meeting of the representatives of every region to track our progress. Suddenly, my region was head and shoulders above everyone else. A director asked, "Could you share with us how you've managed to get everyone on board?" I gulped. The politically correct answer would have been, "We have a collaborative team." Instead I replied honestly, "The only thing I've found to work is command/control."

It's amazing how responsive people are when the one who holds their future in his hand tells them they must either do what they must do or they will be held accountable.

ow that what she calls "the great nonevent" (Y2K) is long gone, Ann, who works for a major international transportation company, is back to spending her days managing her region's multimillion-dollar budget. But she has carried over into budgeting some of the lessons learned in the command/control crisis mode. As she said in the previous chapter, she tries not to yell, not to lose her temper and to be genuinely sympathetic to team members. However, when she (or her boss) is ultimately responsible for an outcome, she makes certain that team members understand their culpability. She tells them: "There will be accountability."

She has learned to "leave it at that, because sometimes what's unsaid is more forceful than what is said."

A Typical Planning Situation

Ann's planning proficiency, while useful in the Y2K command situation, is even more critical in her annual budgeting capacity. In the planning process, she has found that command/control is not the best management method. Here's how she describes the process that works best in this setting:

> Prior to the budget process, we receive an early warning such as: Utilities will increase ten percent, contracted services will increase five percent, etc. Then they'll say we have to come in flat to where we were last year. So something is going to have to give.

At that point, Ann looks at the previous year's budget and then presents the scenario to the various departments for whom she is responsible for budgeting. About her approach to the various departments she says,

> I try to make it as collaborative as I can. It is important that I understand their issues, and it's important to them to believe that I understand their issues. If I were to just say, "This is it, and I don't care what your input is," they would wash their hands of accountability and say to me by their actions, if not their words, "It's not my budget, it's *yours*. You manage it."
>
> So I try to get as much buy-in as I can. I'll start by saying to them, "Tell me what you need to run your business. Give me as much explanation as you can. Understand that I will probably have to come back

and take money or people from you. I will try not to do that. But, knowing that, don't blow smoke, either, because I will find it and then I will consider you a 'smoke blower.' "

There's a lot of interaction back and forth, and sooner or later we get to a number that we can all somewhat live with.

The planning and management principles Ann's budgeting process demonstrates can teach us many lessons.

A Collaborative Effort

She calls her approach to the budget process "consultative management." It's not management by consensus (where the group discusses a matter *ad nauseam* until finally reaching agreement on an outcome after wasting more time and energy than they can afford on the discussion). Neither is it an autocratic, command/control style where what the boss says goes and there is no room for discussion. The consultative style is a corporate middle ground, where interested parties can provide input, but the ultimate authority for the final decision rests in the hands of an "in-charge" person.

Respecting the Input of Others

Since I'm usually a middle-ground kind of person, I find this cooperative style the most comfortable for my day-to-day management responsibilities. Like Ann, I have found it to be the most profitable. To me, it is almost a fairness issue: The people who are most affected by a decision deserve to have input before the decision is made. However, most times the greater good of the organization cannot be best served when special-interest lobbyists are in control of the decision making.

Ann says, "Everybody brings something different to the discussion. I bring concerns from the dollars-and-cents side; the woman in charge of training and culture brings the people element; the individual department heads bring logistic sensitivity." Each of these perspectives is necessary as decisions are made that will have an impact upon the success of the whole organization.

Ann is open and honest with her team: "I encourage your input, but at the end of the day I don't need to find a solution that will make everyone 100 percent happy. I can't do it. But I promise you that I will take your input, I will listen to you, I will understand you and I will do my best within the parameters I have to work with."

Looking Back to Look Forward

Just as Ann begins her number crunching by examining the budgets of the previous years, magazine editorial manager Jodi undertakes her creative work in much the same way. Jodi, who attributes her measure of success as a manager to tireless (sometimes even obsessive) planning, says, "I guess it's the gift of administration at work in me. My idea of being organized is reviewing my database as I plan each issue of the magazine. I find that knowing what happened in the past helps improve the future I'm planning for."

Jodi's process of working through an issue incorporates sitting down with her editorial and design team at the inception of each month's publication planning and at various points along the way. She says, "I am a big believer in 'iron sharpens iron.' When I am open to listening to other members of the team, the final product is improved. People can go so far as to say, 'That's a dumb idea.' I'll listen to them, just like I want them to listen to me when I have a valuable comment to make about their work. If I make a mistake, hopefully someone else on the team will catch it. I can do the same for them."

Another Case Study

The actions of the ancient Persian queen Esther after learning of Haman's plot to annihilate her people provide us with another series of valuable lessons as we seek to become more proficient and productive planners in our own realms of influence. First, let's read two excerpts from the biblical account of her actions:

> The king was sitting on his royal throne in the hall, facing the entrance. When he saw Queen Esther standing in the court, he was pleased with her and held out to her the gold scepter that was in his hand. So Esther approached and touched the tip of the scepter.
>
> Then the king asked, "What is it, Queen Esther? What is your request? Even up to half the kingdom, it will be given you."
>
> "If it pleases the king," replied Esther, "let the king, together with Haman, come today to a banquet I have prepared for him."
>
> "Bring Haman at once," the king said, "so that we may do what Esther asks."

So the king and Haman went to the banquet Esther had prepared. As they were drinking wine, the king again asked Esther, "Now what is your petition? It will be given you. And what is your request? Even up to half the kingdom, it will be granted."

Esther replied, "My petition and my request is this: If the king regards me with favor and if it pleases the king to grant my petition and fulfill my request, let the king and Haman come tomorrow to the banquet I will prepare for them. Then I will answer the king's question." (Esther 5:1-8)

So the king and Haman went to dine with Queen Esther, and as they were drinking wine on that second day, the king again asked,

"Queen Esther, what is your petition? It will be given you. What is your request? Even up to half the kingdom, it will be granted."

Then Queen Esther answered, "If I have found favor with you, O king, and if it pleases your majesty, grant me my life—this is my petition. And spare my people—this is my request. For I and my people have been sold for destruction and slaughter and annihilation. If we had merely been sold as male and female slaves, I would have kept quiet, because no such distress would justify disturbing the king" (7:2-4).

Creative Solution

In several positions that I've held in the publishing industry I've been invited to participate in creative committee meetings. For several years I sat on a publishing board where we made subjective decisions about what kinds of books we would publish, which book proposals to accept (or accept with modifications) and which to reject. I also sat on the marketing committee that wrote fitting and eye-catching titles for more than sixty books per year. All this to say that one of the valuable skills I bring to the workplace is my creativity. Yet I sit in utter amazement as I examine the elaborate plan that Esther created and carried out.

I would never have thought of "buttering up the king" with flattery, food and drink. I'd likely have thrown myself at his feet immediately and begged for my life and that of my loved ones. Instead, Esther demonstrated restraint (which we'll examine in depth in chapter 11) and painstakingly created a nonthreatening, pleasurable atmosphere for the king (whom she knew to be influenced heavily by those things that gave him pleasure and comfort and ego strokes). She recognized that in this atmosphere he would be more open to listen to her request and less apt to be distracted by his growling stomach.

What can we apply from this example? We can think outside the box just as Esther did—we can open ourselves to consider solutions to our own planning dilemmas that might be a little unorthodox, a little out-of-the-everyday. And we can reward those on our teams who do the same. Instead of being suspect of ideas that don't conform in every way to the tried and true way we've always undertaken a task, we can invite the creativity of improving a situation by infusing a fresh perspective or outlook. Creativity can be a great boon to our work plans, just as it was in Esther's case.

Free from Distraction

Esther's creative plan also got the king apart from his usual bevy of yes-men. By taking him aside and making her urgent request in the quiet and privacy of her own quarters, she broke free of the protective barriers she would have encountered had she made the request while Xerxes was sitting on his throne with all of his advisors clamoring for attention.

This reminds me that amid the chaos of events unfolding at work, it is often necessary to take a team member aside—to lunch perhaps or at least to a one-on-one meeting behind closed doors—to discuss an important matter far away from eavesdropping ears or distracting phone calls (a task made more difficult with the proliferation of cell phones and pagers).

Methodical

The next lesson we can draw from Esther's scheme is that she didn't give away the whole plan at one time. She slowly and methodically carried it out. She kept a keen eye on appearances, even down to including (and appearing to honor) her people's most cunning and ruthless enemy, Haman.

"Oh, great king, if it please you, come tonight to dinner in my apartment and bring with you your most trusted advisor Haman" (5:4, author paraphrase). Instead of allowing appearances to honor the cunning and ruthless Haman, I'd probably have choked on the words and fingered the guy right on the spot. Yet Esther bided her time, waiting with patience (not my strong suit) for the right moment, after (not before) the second banquet (not the first).

She went about each request in a systematic and orderly way, treating the king with the respectful deference due his position. Her every action in the king's presence required a dance of precision and she was the model of a practiced dancer, taking each step in its order as the music required it to be performed. (Recall that she had spent a year being coached by the king's eunuch in court etiquette—and she proved herself a skilled learner.) I fancy that she had rehearsed the dance, with all of its intricacies and precise steps, over and over in her head.

I am amazed at Esther's sense of the dramatic. She meted out knowledge a little at a time. She built up the king's expectations to the point where he was so ingratiated to her that he was willing to give her anything she wanted, without restriction or condition.

She also inflated Haman's ego—setting him up for the kill. It was the perfect plan. The irony. The anticipation. The drama. No playwright has ever set up a more perfectly heart-pounding scene. We are sitting rigid with anticipation at that climactic moment when Esther finally blurts out, "Grant me my life . . . and spare my people!" (7:3).

Timely

Obviously God was at work in the timing of Esther's revelation of her nationality. Between the first and second banquets God allowed Xerxes to suffer from insomnia and to call for a reading from the annals of his kingdom (great bedtime reading, don't you think?). How *coincidental* that the reading happened to be from the section that reminded the king of Mordecai's astute and timely warning of the plot to assassinate him. After this reminder, the king was even more disposed to honor and respect Esther's heritage—and the value of all of the Jews to his kingdom.

In the ultimate irony, Haman had the privilege of spending the next day making a show throughout the entire city of Susa, leading his most hated enemy Mordecai through the streets, calling out as he went, "This is a man the king delights in honoring" (see Esther 6:11).

As I read this portion of the narrative, I am reminded that while my inclination may be to rush in and blurt out my desires to my coworkers or even my own staff, more often wisdom dictates patience and a sense of appropriate—sometimes even dramatic—timing.

Well-Prepared

I want to draw one more parallel between our own workplace planning opportunities and the plan Queen Esther devised. She demonstrates the importance of having not only our facts straight but also of preparing our hearts and minds for difficult confrontations. Recall that it took several days of silent meditation (prayer) and fasting for the queen to devise and prepare for this intervention scheme. In this time she skillfully prepared not one but two private banquets fit for the king and his top advisor. It required coordinating a staff of people (who were fasting with her) in this preparation. (Imagine laying out two banquets of temptingly sumptuous foods while you are in the midst of a seventy-two-hour fast!)

The plan also required time-consuming preparation of herself: soaking in her royal bath, applying her royal perfumes and dressing in her royal robes. All these she undertook and accomplished while in an attitude of prayer—of dependence upon God to provide her the resources she needed.

These days, not only do we have the same arsenal of prayer available to us as did such role models as Esther and Dorcas (which I discuss in depth in my book *Praying Like Jesus*), but we also have the collected, time-tested wisdom of God's Word, the Bible, to help prepare us for workplace situations that might seem overwhelming.

Ann says she often turns to the Scriptures when she feels the task to which she is called is more than she can handle. In the Psalms, especially, she finds great encouragement. She quotes Psalm 139:9-10 as an example: "If I take the wings of the morning, and dwell in the uttermost parts of the sea, even there Your hand shall lead me, and Your right hand shall hold me" (NKJV).

> I think of that on the professional level, when I've been dropped into a situation that's beyond my experience or that I'm floundering with. I keep thinking "His right hand will guide me," even though I'm in a strange place and I don't know how to work through it. Even if I don't have anybody else to ask, He will guide me. This ties in to Romans 8:28: "all things work together for good" (KJV). When I'm in a strange place, I'm there for a reason. I'm being guided, being led by the Lord.

When the Responsibility Falls to Me

Ann's observation is consistent with what we observe throughout the Scriptures.

One of the most politically powerful women in the Bible demonstrates for us this pattern of dependence on God as we plan and undertake our work. The woman was Deborah, a judge over all Israel. She lived at a time between the death of Joshua (about 1375 B.C.) and the establishment of the kingdom of Israel (about 1043 B.C.). She was the fourth in a series of twelve judges who ruled Israel, and she was the only woman to hold such a position. She is not only called a judge, but also a prophetess, a representative of God who spoke His words to her nation.

According to the *Parson's Bible Atlas*,

> The judges, usually military leaders, delivered God's people from foreign oppressors. Afterward the victorious judges helped the people maintain their commitment to God. They also settled disputes too difficult for local courts. Deborah was the fourth judge of Israel. Barak was her general. . . .
>
> Deborah clearly was far more assertive and confident than her general, Barak. She issued the call to battle (Judges 4:6); Barak was unwilling to go into battle unless Deborah accompanied him (Judges 4:8). While this was undoubtedly because Deborah, as a prophetess, represented the presence of God, Barak's stand also suggests Deborah's forceful personality and unbounded faith. Deborah finally consented to go with Barak, and the battle began at her command, "Go!" (Judges 4:14).[1]

Under Deborah's direction and with God's supernatural intervention, the ragtag army of Israel defeated the oppressor's well-trained fighting force. As the God-established leader and as God's mouthpiece to the people, Deborah was connected into God's will and His purposes. She and her general Barak would not have succeeded in this daunting undertaking had she not been confident of God's clear word concerning the matter.

I like the *Parson's Bible Atlas* description of Deborah's character as a "forceful personality" of "unbounded faith." Her presence made even a military leader feel more confident, more willing to subject himself to the life-threatening warfare he was anticipating. I think of Deborah as authoritative and, because of that authority, comforting. The people knew they could depend on her to be honest, just, unbiased and unswayed by her own political aspirations.

It has long been my prayer that as I plan and strategize at work as part of a team, I will exhibit the wisdom and creativity of Queen Esther and the genuine care and concern of the judge Deborah. I submit to you that their examples in these areas can offer concrete solutions that will work in your professional life, as well.

Questions for Prayerful Consideration

1. What are my strengths and weaknesses in the area of planning at work?
2. How have I seen different management or team-building styles at work in real-life situations?
3. Which lessons from Esther and Deborah are most applicable to my work situation?

4. What are three specific steps I can take as I seek to grow in my planning and teamwork skills?

Endnote

1. *Parson's Bible Atlas*. Electronic Edition STEP files © Parsons Technology, Inc. 1998. All rights reserved. "Atlas: Deborah, Barak and Shamgar."

Ten

Wise Even under Pressure

We are pressed on every side by troubles, but we are not crushed and broken. We are perplexed, but we don't give up and quit. We are hunted down, but God never abandons us. We get knocked down, but we get up again and keep going. (2 Corinthians 4:8-9; NLT)

Mary's Story: Trainer Prepares Flight Attendants to Handle Pressure

Occasionally, there are times when planes make emergency landings. Most often this is due simply to taking every precaution for safety. But that can be a stress on everyone, especially the flight attendants who are helping passengers in the cabins. So we give flight attendants emergency training every year. During that training we put them into a mock situation where there's an emergency, and then we give them the tools to handle it.

The ones who later go through actual emergencies say it's amazing how much the training kicks in. They find that they're not thinking of the emergency, instead they are concentrating on what needs to be done. When we hear stories like that, we know the training is working.

The stress doesn't really hit them until after the fact. So once the flight has arrived, we always have a management person there to meet them, talk with them and assess how they're doing. The questions we as managers ask at those times are:

- What do you need?
- How are you feeling?
- Are you going to need some time to cope with this?
- Would you like to talk with someone from the Employee Assistance Program?

If they aren't OK to go back in the air right away, we get replacements for them. They need to feel OK.

Sometimes I'll talk to them when they return to their home base, and they'll say they have already forgotten all about the situation. Then I'll say, "OK, just checking."

The goal of our training and our follow-up is that we try to recognize the stresses flight attendants are under and try to come up with ways for them to handle those stresses in a positive way.

*N*ot every profession has such intentional and thorough preparation for its workers to handle everyday stresses as the airline industry. However, if there is one unifying factor in all professions, in all of the settings in which we ply our trades, it is the element of anxiety or strain or stress—whatever you want to call it—that pervades our work lives.

As I plodded through my days in the corporate world, clad in my requisite business blazer, skirt, blouse, scarf, hose and three-inch-heeled pumps, I used to daydream about the day when the stress of the office would give way to the relaxed freedom of self-employment. That is, until I dipped my toes in the frigid waters of the self-employment ocean. Yes, I am free to dress casually on some workdays. And theoretically I can operate according to my own time schedule.

However, rather than stuffing my work in a briefcase at the end of each business day, I operate on the time schedule of each client I serve: I must be available in the office or via my cellular phone throughout the business day in their time zones as well as my own. I find myself juggling the demands of each client as if he were the only one I needed to serve because if I don't serve him at his convenience and on his terms, he'll find someone who will. I also answer to government authorities as I keep accounting records of product and service sales. I pay for my own insurance and plan my own retirement program. I answer phones, stuff mailings, write checks and purchase office products. In the swapping of work environments, I exchanged one brand of anxiety for an equally taxing stressor from a different source.

Whether our work environment is formal or relaxed, whether we are part of a vast team or a one-woman-band, all of us find that our career success and our physical health depend upon whether we are able to manage stress and turn it to our own best advantage.

As the Barometer Rises . . .

Friends of mine have an exceedingly bright child. Though it was evident from his eyes that he understood everything going on around him, he was unable to speak until he was nearly three years old. This frustrated the child to no end. Since he was unable to explain himself, he expressed his frustration by vocalizing high-pitched screams and by aggravated gesturing toward those things he wanted. However, once he had undergone speech therapy and was finally able to express himself, the screams and rough gestures immediately ceased.

Watching this child grow and learn, I saw hints of my own methods of expressing frustration and anger. In times of stress, we all tend to be reduced to our most childish behavior. We want to scream and flail our limbs about in rage when life gets to be more than we can bear.

We can recognize the symptoms as they overtake us. For me it's abdominal spasms that make it painful to take even a shallow breath. It's waking at 3 a.m. with an agitated mind twisting and strangling as if in a swaddling shroud of dread. It's an angry glare that dares anyone to cross my path at risk of his own safety. It's an overreaction in one situation that masks my inability or unwillingness to address the actual source of my frustration, which is unrelated to the circumstance at hand.

For others the symptoms show themselves through sweaty palms, throbbing headaches, racing pulses and dry mouths. Still others externalize the stress. Rather than taking it out on their own bodies they open the pressure valve and spew noxious steam at anyone in their path. These people may express stress through bitter arguments or physical confrontations with people in the workplace or at home.

Whatever the symptoms are for you, every one of us spends seasons of life feeling like a teapot sitting atop a red-hot burner, steam building up and pressing against the interior constraints on all sides until she can no longer contain the pressure. Like that teapot, we all need a valve that opens to release the pent-up pressure.

Fortunately, just like the flight attendants who receive crisis training, we too can take steps toward learning to manage our stress and express our frustration in useful ways.

All it will take is time, concerted effort and practice in making use of an arsenal of skills that are already at our disposal.

Prescription for Stress

Dr. Jenny, who has studied all of the theoretical causes and effects of stress upon our bodies, still struggles with her own pressure points—which her children recognize, even when she doesn't see them coming. Jenny offers this scenario as an example:

> My daughter Rebecca came up to me the other morning. We had been having one of those mornings—you know the ones. Everybody's tense because although we all know what we're supposed to be doing, nobody's doing it. Things were getting a little more tense, and a little more, and . . . that's when Rebecca came up to me. She looked at me with these big eyes and said, "Mommy, I think you need to go talk to God."
>
> You know what? She was right. If I can get away and tell God, I can leave it there. I climb up in Father's lap and tell on 'em all. Then I feel like, "OK, I've told You; now it's Your problem," and I can walk away refreshed.

Medically speaking, Jenny notes the traditionally accepted methods of handling stress profitably. She reminds us:

> Talk to someone who won't just let you off the hook, but will offer counsel to keep you on the right path;
>
> Give your mind a chance to clear by exercising—especially by taking a long walk;

And be sure to take care of your body by getting a good night's sleep and eating a balanced diet.

But the prescription she writes for herself is a combination that adds to all of these a healthy dose of faith: "I find it's a good thing to get out and walk and talk to God—to combine the exercise element with talking to the Someone who really won't let me off the hook. This is what works for me."

She says we can also provide a pressure valve for other people as we see them stressing out. She tells of a pastor friend who ministered to her in this way during her residency: "He'd hunt me down wherever I was in the hospital and just take a minute to say, 'I want you to know that I care about you.' That did so much to make me feel like I was going to make it through the day."

Today, her husband Donny plays a role as encourager and pressure reliever in Jenny's life. She recalls many occasions when she would be with a patient in an examination room and she'd see a sheet of paper from her prescription pad slide in under the door. When she'd pick it up, she'd see Donny's signature below a series of X's and O's. "Those little bitty acts of love are so small that we may not even take them into account as we do them, but I know I'll never forget the pastor coming to find me or Donny slipping those notes under the door," she says.

Stress and the Type-A Person

Accountant Joan is a high-energy woman. She speaks quickly. She acts decisively. And she sometimes feels as though stress follows her around. It took living through a shattering divorce, her daughter's spinal surgeries and her own life-threatening medical crisis for Joan to learn to be quiet, to relax and to "de-stress" herself. It did not come naturally. Here's how she describes what works for her:

> Some days were so hectic that I would just go in my office, leave the lights off (hoping that nobody would see me and that I'd be alone for a couple of minutes) and close my eyes. I'd try to commune with the Lord. I'd ask Him, "Lord, am I doing the right thing? Did I say the right thing to that person? What should I be doing now?" One of the first things I learned is that I need to pull myself away from everybody and get alone with the Lord. I don't know how anybody gets through a day without turning to Him.
>
> Because I can't come home and just turn off all of the hectic chaos of the day, I have learned that Bible reading, even if it means just carving out five or ten minutes, helps me calm down before I go to bed. I subscribe to several magazines, including *Guideposts* and *Leadership*. Reading these before I go to bed helps too. I prop myself up on a big pillow, turn on the indoor waterfall my kids bought me for Christmas, put a symphonic CD into the stereo and read from the Bible or one of these magazines, so that the last thing I'm thinking about before I go to sleep is God-centered. The sound of the waterfall is soothing; the Scripture reminders put life in the right perspective for me. These things taken together calm me so I can sleep peacefully.

High school administrator Elizabeth has a similar pattern of de-stressing herself. "On the days when I come home aggravated, I take a half hour to myself, sit back and look at something else to change the tone of my day. I might read. Or sit peacefully. Eventually it all calms down. Sometimes it reappears the next day. But I try to remind myself that a week from now this problem will be over and probably forgotten."

Listen to an oft-quoted passage from the book of Philippians: "Whatever is true, whatever is noble, whatever is right, whatever is pure, whatever is lovely, whatever is admirable—if anything is excellent or praiseworthy—think about such things" (4:8). This sounds remarkably similar to the real-life application Elizabeth and Joan have seen work in their own circumstances. Don't you just sit back in amazement when biblical principles turn out to offer the most sound and sensible counsel for our daily lives?

Diffusing the Pressure

Another principle of dealing effectively with the things that cause our anxiety meters to approach the red zone is being honest with ourselves about the situation and about how we might work to better it.

Jodi, a self-supporting single mother of a preteen daughter, finds that home conflicts often translate into stress at work. So several years ago she transitioned from an inflexible job to a position in a nonprofit organization where there is an openness to family issues. "Where I work now, my daughter can come into the office with me if she is sick or off from school," Jodi says. "She can sit beside me and read a book while I work, and my boss doesn't mind." Jodi is also able to work out of her home several days a week. These factors make it worthwhile for Jodi to work in a nonprofit setting, even if she could receive bigger financial benefits in the profit sector. She has dealt with the stress of motherhood by making a measured choice to put her daughter's care above financial considerations.

Jodi also says honesty and grace can go a long way toward diffusing stressful situations. She offers this example:

> The other day someone sent me a three-page, single-spaced e-mail complaint letter about an error we had made. He was clearly angry about many things. But in response, instead of addressing every individual concern he had expressed in the letter, I sent him an e-mail greeting card that said, "I'm sorry; we made a mistake." That's all it said. This diffused the situation for me and for the other person. In fact, the next time I saw him, he brought a small gift to me and offered his own apology.
>
> Problems like these come up in the course of a day. Rather than stressing out over them, I try to handle one at a time, thinking each through, carrying it before the Lord. When the stress won't dissipate I can hear the Lord saying to me, "Sit down and read My Word, then let this go."
>
> Humor helps too, as well as being gracious—as I tried to be in sending the apology card to the man who wrote the e-mail complaint.

Jodi's operating principles are consistent with scriptural admonitions. I think of a message written by the Apostle Paul to one of his coworkers in the church at Philippi: "I plead with Euodia and I plead with Syntyche to agree with each other in the Lord. Yes, and I ask you, loyal yokefellow, help these women who have contended at my side in the cause of the gospel" (Philippians 4:2-3). There is no place in the body of Christ for sniping at one another. It has always bothered me that it was two women—Euodia and Syntyche—who were singled out as being contentious and bringing dissension into God's household.

When I was in high school, I spent a summer touring the country with a Christian singing group. One of the criteria we had to meet before the tour was memorizing a list of Scripture passages. Most of them related to ministry we would have as we prayed with young people who would come to the altar after our concerts. The list included the plan of salvation found in Romans, sometimes called the "Romans Road," verses on assurance of salvation, holy living, praying for physical healing, etc.[1]

But one required memory verse was selected just for us. It was Philippians 2:14: "Do everything without complaining or arguing." All these years later, I still recall that sound, biblical de-stressing principle. (I recall it, but alas, I don't always remember to apply it.) Our complaining, grousing and fussing do nothing constructive toward resolving a difficult circumstance—in fact, they only serve to compound most problems. When we learn the lesson of Euodia and Syntyche, we take a giant step forward in diffusing the stress in our own lives, as well as in the lives of those around us.

Esther's Plan of Attack

So far, we've seen what works in our modern lives, but we could also benefit from stress-busting principles that have proven practical over the millennia. We find several of these in the life of that wise young queen, Esther.

Imagine the stress this woman would have felt over the course of her young life: She is orphaned and then taken in by her elder cousin. While still a young girl, presumably a teenager, she is torn from the only family she has known and forced into a harem as just another one of a gaggle of pretty young maidens. When she rises to the top (as cream will do) she is given a beautiful apartment and a bevy of servants. However, she does not have the undivided attention of her husband. She is isolated from her surrogate father and can receive word from and about him only through a trusted servant. Through this means she learns that her people are going to be slaughtered if she doesn't do something about it. She quickly realizes that *doing something about it* could just cost her her life.

Do you feel her neck muscles constricting? Her nerves straining? Her pulse racing? Take a moment to imagine experiencing Esther's stress. Doesn't it feel similar to the stress you and I experience? Once we can relate to the pressure Esther is feeling, we can examine her responses and learn from her wise choices.

Assess the Situation

Do we see her stuffing her feelings inside or lashing out at the servants around her? Certainly not. Instead we see Esther snap into crisis mode. She analyzed the situation and wisely concocted a tenuous but workable plan. This action offers one of the first principles of handling stress that we can learn from Esther—namely, that there comes a time when we must look for aspects of a situation we can control, and then act to control them. Simply worrying and mulling over the problem does not move us any closer to a conclusion. Only well-thought-through action can bring a solution.

Talk It Over with God

Next, we see that because the path Esther determined to take was fraught with danger, she began with fasting and (presumably) prayer. As Joan and Jenny reminded us earlier in this chapter, turning first to God as we face difficult circumstances and daily choices is a foundational coping mechanism.

Share the Burden

But Esther didn't pray alone—she delegated part of that responsibility to others—to her servants (those who were not directly involved in the problem, but could become part of the solution) and to the entire Jewish community (those who had no control over the solution but were most affected by the problem). Delegation is another of the keys to handling stress, because it reminds us that we are not acting alone. We can share the burden of performing a task with colleagues or with those individuals who work for us. It requires asking for help and trusting those to whom we delegate to work with us and on our behalf; it also presumes our availability to become stress-busters in their lives at some future date. But it does take a portion of the burden off our shoulders during our most tense times.

As believers in Christ, we are part of a community, a family. When one hurts, all hurt. When one is suffering, all desire to pitch in and alleviate the burden. Prayer is one of those ways we can all become involved in shouldering the burdens and de-stressing our fellow believers.[2]

Control What You Can

A final lesson in stress busting that we can find in Esther's wise handling of her predicament is that she chose her battleground. She didn't lash out at Haman in the courts of the king. In fact, she didn't attack Haman at all. That would have been pointless. Instead, she pled her case directly to the one person who could solve the problem—incidentally, he was also the one most inclined to help her. Remember the principle of controlling those things you can? Esther did that in choosing the timing and location of her confrontation. She was composed, prepared, even "prayed-up" before she spoke. There is no hint of reactionism in her plan. She is calm and cautious and methodical. She brings the conversation to her turf and she makes the setting as comfortable and welcoming as possible for the king. If she is feeling the pressure, if indeed her pulse is racing and her palms are sweaty, she is careful not to show it.

This reminds me of the way Paul advises us to approach life's ups and downs. In Philippians, he writes: "Let your gentleness be evident to all. The Lord is near" (4:5); and "Do not be anxious about anything, but in everything, by prayer and petition, with thanksgiving, present your requests to God" (4:6). He concludes by reminding us that when we have done these things, "the peace of God, which transcends all understanding, will guard [our] hearts and [our] minds in Christ Jesus" (4:7). Overall, these are not a bad prescription for handling the stressful situations that barge into our well-ordered lives: Be gentle, be aware of God's presence, be at peace as we entrust Him with our concerns and be on guard against the temptation to worry needlessly. That just might work!

Questions for Prayerful Consideration

1. What are the top five stressors in my life?
2. Once I have carried these stress-causing areas of my life to God in prayer, how will I remind myself to leave them with Him?
3. Which of these stressors can I control? How will I do this?
4. Which of these stressors require a plan of action? How will I act in each case?
5. How can I help alleviate stress in the lives of my staff? my colleagues? my boss? my husband or other family members?

Endnotes

1. The Romans Road is a designation for a series of verses in the book of Romans that describes the entire process of salvation; these include: Romans 3:23; 6:23; and 10:9-10.
2. For a year's worth of suggestions on how to pray for yourself and for fellow believers, pick up a copy of my book, *Praying Like Jesus* (Chicago, IL: Moody Press, 2001).

Eleven

Demonstrates Restraint

David said to Abigail, "Praise be to the LORD, the God of Israel, who has sent you today to meet me. May you be blessed for your good judgment and for keeping me from bloodshed this day and from avenging myself with my own hands." (1 Samuel 25:32-33)

Carrie's Story: Corporate Manager Restores Employee

I once had an employee who didn't exercise personal restraint with her words. She would work hard and well for a while, then without warning she would spew a verbal tirade hotter than molten lava. At the end of each eruption, she would be meek and mild again. For a while—for better or worse—I was able to shield her from the consequences of her out-of-control emotions. But one day when I was out of the office, Vesuvius erupted, and the lava flowed right to my boss's feet. He was furious, paging me out of my meeting and demanding that I *do something* about her. Translation: He wanted me to begin termination proceedings.

After allowing my boss's initial anger to subside, I pleaded her case and offered the alternative of my setting up a series of coaching sessions with her. He was skeptical but agreed to allow my idea a short trial. Together my employee and I identified the problems that were causing her anger and worked out practical methods to overcome them.

To my knowledge, she never knew how close she was to unemployment. Despite my own anger and frustration, I chose to withhold that information from her, sure it would only exacerbate the situation. Instead, I impressed upon her in firm but sympathetic terms that this behavior was inappropriate for the workplace. To her credit, when she came to understand that there are consequences to acting without self-control, she worked diligently to restrain her tantrums and to use the tools I taught her to express her emotions in more appropriate and beneficial ways.

Carrie, for several years a corporate middle-manager, looks back with some pride on the fact that she made what she says was a "good call" in restraining her own anger and instead turning it into something useful by offering to teach her employee the life skills it takes to succeed in the workplace.

She says she has had many opportunities to put her personal restraint to the test, as she has withstood the often-conflicting pressures coming from her needy staff, demanding upper management and a job where successes are difficult to measure. "Sometimes I succeed, and sometimes I wish I had done better," she says. "It's easier to let loose and say exactly what I'm thinking. But we live in a civilized world and that isn't always the best way to solve a situation—it certainly isn't the best way to see that my views will get a positive hearing."

Just what is this idea of personal restraint, and why is it so lacking—and yet so necessary—in our modern, civilized world?

Maintaining Our Cool

The list of synonyms for restraint and self-control is long and telling. Restraint is, among other things: composure, coolness, unflappability, steadiness, calmness. Restraint is not panic, hysteria or immoderation. Road rage is not self-control. Neither are school shootings or the inclination to "go postal" when events don't go our way at work. Rather, diplomacy and tactful negotiation among individuals whose interests differ demonstrate restraint at its best. These examples embody the concepts of fairness, respect and peace, as opposed to allowing our rawest, most base and self-serving instincts to rule our actions.

Believers in Christ receive frequent reminders from New Testament writers that self-control is among the most desired and necessary qualities in God's eyes. In fact, the trait is listed as the last of the nine fruits that the Spirit of God grows in the lives of Christians (Galatians 5:22-23). This desirable fruit is contrary to the natural tendency of humanity, whose inborn traits include such antisocial tendencies as: "hatred, discord, jealousy, fits of rage, selfish ambition . . . and envy." (Don't believe me? See 5:20-21 for the complete list of horrid traits that are innate to unredeemed humanity.)

The writer of Proverbs likens the antithesis of self-control to "a city whose walls are broken down" (25:28). Through this analogy, the voice of wisdom reminds us that self-control is a wall of protection; when that wall comes down we are defenseless against any enemy who seeks our destruction. Similarly, the psalmist challenges us: "Do not be like a senseless horse or mule that needs a bit and bridle to keep it under control" (32:9, NLT). The implication is that when we are out of control, our loving and just God will use every means necessary to bring us back under control—even if it means subjecting us to the painful harnesses of common farm animals. (Now there's one experience I would prefer not to endure!)

As necessary as restraint is to our participation in a civilized society, it is difficult to maintain. Divorce attorney Christina is one of those who deals with individuals at times when their emotions are so frayed and their nerves so stripped of any protective coating that they often allow themselves to run wild. "I don't think any lawyer is equipped to deal with people who are going through an emotional crisis. At those times people are more contentious, less reasonable. They say and do things that aren't in the best interests of their family or themselves. During divorce proceedings people are often their own worst self-sabotagers," she says.

Christina's observation is a good reminder to us. When we are at our most vulnerable—when we are hurt, angry, disappointed, rejected, disillusioned or stressed out—restraint is more necessary than ever, even though it may be nearly impossible to muster at those moments because our reserves are already scant.

Christina constantly reminds herself to maintain her own cool, even when her clients are allowing themselves the short-lived luxury of spinning out of control. "Because of the nature of the work I do, I need to have restraint or things will snowball out of control. Without restraint I cannot better a situation," she says. But with restraint, Christina is aware that she can become for her clients and adversaries the voice of reason, spreading a layer of balm that soothes inflamed nerves. The fact that she works toward this brand of calm resolution makes Christina a sought-after attorney, whose pursuit of truth and fairness seeks out the best interests of all parties in a difficult situation.

The Temptation to Mouth Off

At the other extreme from Christina's calmness is the individual who does allow herself the luxury of verbally lambasting others. As we will see in a moment, even if in the right, the person who loses control will come away from a dispute as the loser. She will have forfeited her own self-respect while damaging a relationship—perhaps irreparably.

Being godly is my friend Ann's primary life goal. She has asked the Lord to correct her with "a two-by-four on the head" whenever she gets out of line. Nevertheless, Ann offers this self-deprecating story as an example of righteous indignation gone awry.

> A fellow manager came into my office. She was upset about a decision I had made. She was yelling and screaming and hollering. I'm usually impervious to that; I've grown a bit of a shell to shield me from angry colleagues. So, while I tried to be sympathetic, I told her I couldn't make a different decision.
>
> Then she proceeded to string together some words I had never heard before in my life. They were a list of profane words that included using the Lord's name in a *terrible* way. To say I was deeply offended would be an understatement.
>
> Now, I don't lose my temper often; but when I do, I get this red flash. I feel like my head is going to explode. That's what happened that day. I slammed my hands down on my desk, pushed back and yelled, "Get out of my office right now!"

She started floundering, and her face got red. "What did I do?"

I said, "You know what you did. I will not listen to that in my office. Get out of here before I do something terrible!"

She got up and marched away. But the minute she cleared my door, the two-by-four fell. I argued with it; after all, I had a right to be angry. This was a righteous call. But I knew deep down that I was as wrong as I could be—I didn't have to like what she said, but I must handle her in a loving way. To make it worse, I had been trying to witness to her.

I immediately got up from my chair and went to her office. Wouldn't you know it? In that little slice of time she had left for the day—and it was Friday. I lived through the whole weekend repenting.

On Monday I went to her and said, "What you said was horrible, but I wasn't right to act toward you as I did." She accepted the apology. I'm sure she's forgotten about it. But what's that in James? Once you've said something you can never quite get it back.

Ann's allusion is to the writings of the Apostle James, who tells us: "a tiny rudder makes a huge ship turn wherever the pilot wants it to go, even though the winds are strong. So also, the tongue is a small thing, but what enormous damage it can do" (James 3:4-5, NLT). Earlier in the chapter James issues this challenge: "We all make many mistakes, but those who control their tongues can also control themselves in every other way" (3:2, NLT).

I admire Ann's transparency for sharing that story. When she told it to me, I asked her how she wishes she had responded at that moment of blinding fury. After thinking for only a moment she said, "I would have said quietly, maybe laced with a little humor, 'You know I don't like swearing at all. And that particular combination is offensive beyond belief. You are taking in vain the name of Someone who is very dear to me.' I wish I would have taken the opportunity to tell her why I found it so offensive."

Ann's preferred response illustrates how much better we could make many situations if we were to restrain our tongues from their first inclination to lash out, if we were to restrict our actions to only those that spread healing balm over a festering gash of misunderstanding.

A Perfect Example

We have no better example for our lives than that of Jesus Christ. In the face of the jeers and mockings and verbal tirades of the rulers of His day, Jesus demonstrated the ultimate restraint. Bruised and already battered, Jesus was dragged before the highest religious authority on earth, the high priest, and subjected to a mock trial, piled high with the stench of half-truths and flat-out lies. "Then the high priest stood up and said to Jesus, 'Well, aren't you going to answer these charges? What do you have to say for yourself?' But Jesus remained silent" (Matthew 26:62-63, NLT).

To add to our cultural understanding of these events and the significance of the complete control Jesus maintained upon His own conduct in the face of the ultimate injustice, let's examine the scene from the perspective of Alfred Edersheim's *The Life and Times of Jesus the Messiah*, written in 1883. Edersheim explains:

> Hatred, fanaticism, and unscrupulous Eastern exaggeration would readily misrepresent and distort certain sayings of Christ, or falsely impute others to Him. But it was altogether too hasty and excited an assemblage, and the witnesses contradicted themselves so grossly, or their testimony so notoriously broke down, that for very shame such trumped-up charges had to be abandoned. And to this result the majestic calm of Christ's silence must have greatly contributed. On directly false and contradictory testimony it must be best not to cross-examine at all, not to interpose, but to leave the false witness to destroy itself.[1]

When Jesus did respond to the high priest, it was only after Caiaphas charged Him in the name of the Living God, to tell whose Son He was. Edersheim explains the necessity and content of Jesus' response: "No doubt or hesitation could here exist. Solemn, emphatic, calm, majestic, as before had been His silence, was now His speech."[2] Jesus answered the priest respectfully and honestly when charged by the name of God to do so. He maintained this cool and composed disposition throughout that tragic night and day. Edersheim describes Christ as "majestic in His silence, majestic in His speech; unmoved by threats to speak, undaunted by threats when He spoke."[3]

Later that day, even the pompous Pilate stood amazed at Jesus' decision not to answer the accusations leveled against Him. In a beautiful analogy, Edersheim explains: "It was as if the surging of the wild waves broke far beneath against the base of the rock, which, untouched, reared its head far aloft to the heavens. But as He stood in the calm silence of Majesty, Pilate greatly wondered."[4]

How often have you and I felt those surging, wild waves breaking against us? I can tell you the time and place, down to the minute, of my most recent battering by the surging waves. My temptation is, in my own strength, to do as Ann did, to lash out, to strike first—or at least to strike back in my own (or God's) defense. And yet, by maintaining this majestic silence when provoked, and this majestic speech when necessary, Jesus sets for us a higher ideal—an example we can attain only when we operate in His strength, empowered and indwelt by His Spirit.[5]

Does it come naturally? No. But when our heart's prayer is for the God who lives in us to be in control of our responses, of our tongues, of our emotions and our energies, He will be faithful to equip us to withstand the pressure.

> But remember that the temptations that come into your life are no different from what others experience. And God is faithful. He will keep the temptation from becoming so strong that you can't stand up against it. When you are tempted, he will show you a way out so that you will not give in to it. (1 Corinthians 10:13, NLT)

We can be at peace in the knowledge that God will be true to His Word; our responsibility is to look for His "way out" and then choose to take it.

A Helping of God's Peace

"Blessed are the peacemakers," Jesus said (Matthew 5:9). Why? Because peacemakers will be recognized as sons and daughters of the Prince of Peace. Peacemakers are by nature controlled. Their motives are the opposite of self-serving. They are those who look out for the best interests of others, who seek common ground and work creatively to bring about calmly administered solutions to difficult problems.

In the last chapter we examined the restrained and measured response Queen Esther had to the turmoil going on around her. And as we finish the retelling of her story in the next chapter, we'll see that the result of her peaceful demeanor and restrained action was the saving of an entire nation. But I'd also like to mention two other Bible women who reined in their emotions and worked to better a situation.

The first woman is Jochebed, Moses' mother. Likely, you've heard her story since Sunday school days; you've seen her in your mind's eye weaving one papyrus reed after another into a basket, coating it with tar and placing her helpless infant son and the basket in the Nile River. But have you felt the broken heart of a mother who must walk away and leave her child in the hands of an unseen God? Have you watched her muster the self-discipline to kiss that little cheek for presumably the last time, stand from a crouching position and walk away? God rewarded Jochebed's restraint and obedience by safely returning the child Moses to her care—but she couldn't have known that would happen when she blinked back her tears and placed the baby in the reedy waters (see Exodus 2). I doubt that my restraint reservoir would have been sufficient for Jochebed's task.

The second woman I'd like to mention is Abigail. We began this chapter with a quote from First Samuel 25 where

King David commends Abigail for the restraint she modeled for him. Here's a synopsis of her story: Abigail is a wise, insightful woman. She is married to a burly, self-important fool, Nabal. (Don't believe me; read the Bible's description of him yourself [1 Samuel 25:3].) David and his warriors, while hiding from King Saul's ambushes, come across Abigail's husband's flocks. The warriors protect the flocks from bandits and wild animals. In payment, they ask for a quantity of food and water from Nabal. He refuses, unbeknownst to Abigail. David becomes furious and determines to slaughter Nabal and his household. Abigail, hearing a report of these events from a servant, assembles a quantity of food and goes to David herself. She not only restrains her own fear and anger, but she also exudes calmness and diplomacy. As all good negotiators, her presence introduces a contagious coolness of temper. Listen to her words:

> I accept all blame in this matter, my lord. Please listen to what I have to say. I know Nabal is a wicked and ill-tempered man; please don't pay any attention to him. He is a fool, just as his name suggests. But I never even saw the messengers you sent.
>
> Now, my lord, as surely as the LORD lives and you yourself live, since the LORD has kept you from murdering and taking vengeance into your own hands, let all your enemies be as cursed as Nabal is. And here is a present I have brought to you and your young men. Please forgive me if I have offended in any way. The LORD will surely

> reward you with a lasting dynasty, for you are
> fighting the LORD's battles. And you have not
> done wrong throughout your entire life. . . .
>
> When the LORD has done all he promised and
> has made you leader of Israel, don't let this be a
> blemish on your record. Then you won't have to
> carry on your conscience the staggering burden of
> needless bloodshed and vengeance. (1 Samuel
> 25:24-31, NLT)

Let's examine the skillful diffusing and negotiating techniques Abigail models. She acknowledges David's right to be
angry. She apologizes for the injustice, even though she was
not directly responsible for it. She rights the wrong by providing a generous supply of provisions. Then she tells David
that she recognizes his authority as the future (already-
anointed) king of Israel, and she reminds him in a gentle yet
authoritative way that as God's man he ought not act rashly
or repay evil for evil.

Even the masterful negotiating of former Secretary of State
Madeleine Albright (whom we met in the opening of this book)
couldn't improve on this technique or hope for a better outcome than the one Abigail's wisdom brought about.

What was the result of Abigail's negotiations? David's anger was assuaged. He restrained himself from vengeance and
commended her wisdom. Then when Nabal found out how
close he was to disaster, he suffered a seizure; within days he
died. David, remembering the good effect Abigail had on
him, married her himself.

Note that Abigail brings out the best in David, which is one of the greatest benefits of remaining in control of our words and deeds. Like Carrie early in the chapter, as each of us models self-control in her sphere of influence, others cannot help but be influenced. Carrie called her boss to a higher standard—challenging him to temper anger with grace, and she called upon her employee to learn a skill that would benefit the entire work team. All parties were challenged to grow just because of one peacemaker.

Similarly, when we submit ourselves to the control of the Spirit of the God of all peace, we will be sought after and respected because of our placid demeanor in tense times. We too will bring out the best in those around us. James 3:17-18 says,

> But the wisdom that comes from heaven is first of all pure. It is also peace loving, gentle at all times, and willing to yield to others. It is full of mercy and good deeds. It shows no partiality and is always sincere. And those who are peacemakers will plant seeds of peace and reap a harvest of goodness. (NLT)

A "harvest of goodness" is what I want in my life and in the lives of my employees, colleagues, superiors, clients, friends, church and family. So I find myself asking God again to help me maintain a calm, Holy Spirit-controlled demeanor like the ones modeled by Jochebed, Abigail and especially Jesus Christ. If I maintain such a calm, I will be a worker for peace and I will be recognized as a child of His in a world where people have become "lovers of themselves, lovers of money, boastful, proud, abusive . . . unforgiving, slanderous, without self-control, brutal

. . . treacherous, rash, conceited, lovers of pleasure rather than lovers of God" (2 Timothy 3:2-4).

Questions for Prayerful Consideration

1. As I take an honest assessment of my recent conduct, what are some specific circumstances where I have allowed myself to react in anger rather than responding in a controlled manner or remaining silent?

2. Looking back on those situations, how would I have *liked* to respond?

3. What are some of the ways I learned (or relearned) from the good examples of Christ and His followers that I can become a peacemaker or a good negotiator to diffuse difficult situations?

4. What are three specific things I can pray for as I seek to become a model of God's peace to the people I encounter in the community, at work, at church and at home?

Endnotes

1. *The Life and Times of Jesus the Messiah* Electronic STEP edition; Edersheim, Alfred; Book V: The Cross and the Crown, Chapter XIII Section 2. [Author's note: This is one of the best researched texts that helps us understand the context, culture and significance of each scene of Jesus' life.]

2. Ibid.

3. Ibid.

4. Ibid. Section 3.

5. For more biblical guidance here, read Paul's description of the Spiritual Armor available to believers in Ephesians 6:11-17.

Twelve

Willingly Communicates Information

But the servant replied, "Look, in this town there is a man of God; he is highly respected, and everything he says comes true. Let's go there now. Perhaps he will tell us what way to take." (1 Samuel 9:6)

Tammy's Story: Journalist Sees the Best and Worst Communicators at Work

I find I always most appreciate supervisors and coworkers who are up front about what they want. Here's an example of what I don't mean: Just this week I witnessed a situation where the director of a department blew up at a subordinate over a situation he knew about, but she didn't. In a meeting, she tried to voice an opinion on how to approach upcoming changes. After repeatedly interrupting her, he began shouting—even shoving his finger in her face. She wisely said nothing during the tirade, but when he finally finished she calmly voiced her concerns and continued in a civil tone through the remainder of the meeting.

When it was over and everyone else had left, he apologized profusely, then explained the situation that was causing him such consternation. But that was *his* problem. Rather than precipitating a scene, he could have let her speak, then after the meeting privately explained the situation. Had he done this, he would have attained a more profitable result.

I can still recall someone who handled these situations in a far better way. He was a county administrator, now deceased, who seemed to approach every issue with calm diplomacy. Not that he never felt strongly about things, but he was always careful to consider both sides of an issue and let proponents of each side have their say. He rarely held back information unless it was an absolute necessity, rarely raised his voice, always expressed himself with well-crafted, reasonable arguments and never berated people. I think I only saw him behave rudely to somebody once, and that guy, frankly, had asked for it. But my even-tempered colleague couldn't stand it; within five minutes he approached the guy and gave him all the information he'd asked for.

*A*s a reporter on the political beat for many years, and later as a public relations writer and editor, Tammy could tell some stories about the do's and don'ts of communicating our desires and expressing our concerns. Recalling the faces of the two men whose communicating styles she describes above, she says, "What can we learn from them? *Don't be reactionary!*"

That advice, neatly packaged, could go a long way toward calming circumstances and ultimately toward successfully communicating our goals, ambitions, concerns and triumphs among our fellow workers.

The Challenge of Getting Our Point Across

This ought to be the easiest chapter for me to write. Rene the nurse may be the most appropriate person to teach us how to be understanding and kind at work; corporate-minded Ann might be the most qualified to teach us how to navigate the office-ship through adverse winds of change; Dr. Jenny may be the most capable woman to remind us of the importance of handling stress in medically acceptable ways. But I am a communicator. It's the area in which I obtained my degrees. It's the discipline that I've studied and practiced for the better part of two decades. It's the subject of dozens of dog-eared volumes that line the walls of my office/library. And yet it is an area where I still struggle, because communication is a two-way street. It is speaking; but it is also listening. It is framing a message so that it will be understood by an audience; but it is also working to understand the message being conveyed by another person. It is words; and as Rene reminded us in chapter 5, it is getting beyond words to interpret the intent of the communicator's heart.

In the rooms outside and above my office as I write, a textbook example of a communication biosphere is in operation. My office is (currently) in the lower level of my parents' home—a home that is undergoing a reconstruction project of gargantuan proportions. In the biosphere outside my closed (but not soundproofed) doors, a crew of workers—all first-generation immigrants of Eastern European descent—is working to accomplish the addition and remodeling that our very-American architect set to blueprints at our explicit direction. The experiment of communicating with our architect, which took place ten months ago, was quite a challenge—and we were all fluent in English (although in reality he spoke only the specialized English dialect of *architectese*, a variation of the language with which we had to make ourselves familiar on the fly).

But the challenge today is that the work crew, all tradesmen and specialists in their technical fields (a plumber, an electrician, several carpenters, a heating/air-conditioning contractor and an assemblage of hard-working laborers), speak only the language of their native lands. Nevertheless, there are some concepts that *simply must* be communicated between us—such as "Pardon me, but I believe you just stuck your entire boot-clad leg through our family room ceiling" or "Correct me if I'm wrong, but I don't think the plan calls for a waterfall over the opening for the new stairway." You know, trivial matters.

However, except for the Polish equivalents of *please* and *thank you*, which we have learned to say (but not spell) quite recently, my family and I do not speak their language.

This microcosm of life has served as a vivid reminder of the common barriers to communication we all face in the workplace and of some of the ways we can break free of their constraints. My dad, in particular, has come to realize that no matter how slowly he may speak, or how loudly he may raise his voice, communication will not occur when two parties are speaking different languages. Similarly, we've all learned to strip our messages down to their clearest and simplest terms—eliminating all unnecessary adjectives, adverbs and modifiers; forgetting everything we've ever learned about compound-complex sentence structure—if we are to speak directly to our tradesmen.

We've also learned the value of gesturing, of the grade-school skill of show and tell and of drawing simple pictures when all else fails. And we've come to depend heavily on two individuals in the team: the two tradesmen who speak both languages. When either of these two is on site, he is able to translate our wishes to the workers and the workers' responses back to us.

Communication Differences

Why is the issue of communication raised in a book that is examining the character and integrity of a godly woman in the secular marketplace? Primarily because how we communicate has a direct impact upon our reputations, our advancement and our interpersonal relationships at work, as well as in every other arena of life. And, as women, our communication tends to differ significantly from that of our male colleagues.

I'm not being sexist when I make these comments. I'm being realistic. Don't take my word for it. Look no further than the *New York Times* Best-seller List. The book *Men Are from Mars, Women Are from Venus* written by talk-show circuit regular John Gray, Ph.D., has sold more than 6 million copies in the United States, and millions more in at least forty languages around the world.[1] The book's premise? Men and women have different communication styles; these styles are so divergent that we might as well have been born on two different planets.

Tammy offers this observation of the differences she sees played out between the men and women (most of whom are professional communicators) in her office: "Absolutely men and women differ in the ways they communicate. Men tend to deal more in facts and figures and quick retorts, while women are more willing to consider details."

Journalism professor Holly adds her own observations gleaned from years in newspaper and magazine management and corporate public relations.

> We need to take a cue from our male colleagues without trying to imitate them. No, we don't have to talk about football or laugh at questionable jokes to fit in. Neither must we wear pinstripe suits. But we do need to pay attention to our body language and measure it against our male coworkers.
>
> Too often we women wrap ourselves up in our arms, cross our legs and assume a tight position—as if we hope no one will notice our presence. Then, when we become animated, our voices rise in pitch, we talk too fast and we tend to make overly dramatic gestures with our hands to underscore our point. In contrast, men make controlled, clipped gestures. Their lower voices convey steadiness, reliability, unwavering strength.

I'm glad Holly reminds us we don't have to be exactly like men at work, but rather in becoming aware of the differences, we can control the way we are perceived in their eyes. If I want to convey steadiness or strength, I can tone down the pitch and volume of my voice. If I want to convey a controlled demeanor, I can rein in my gestures (which, because of my Italian heritage, tend to be a bit over the top). I don't have to do this, but I make a conscious decision in certain work settings to trade my right to unbridled self-expression for the right to be heard, understood and respected for my relevant opinions.

Another female inclination that Holly calls to our attention is our tendency to turn statements of fact into open-ended questions, leaving room for debate on issues that do not warrant discussion. She explains:

> Rather than saying: "I'm in favor of extending the contract," we say, "I think we should extend the contract, don't you?" Or, rather than announcing, "Let's break for lunch and discuss this at 1 p.m." we say, "Is anyone hungry? Shall we talk about this after lunch?"

Why do we do this? Holly observes that often it is related to our need for approval. We do crave approval. We need validation—for ourselves and our ideas. Perhaps this is because it hasn't been that many years since our opinions were not validated in many offices. Perhaps it relates to the glass ceiling that continues to exist in certain organizations—allowing us to climb to certain heights but not to attain the summit because of our gender.

Although we'd like to think otherwise, we'll still encounter some men at work who'd rather we weren't there. Although she is only in her thirties, Tammy says, "This may sound chauvinistic, but there are still a lot of men in management positions who react to women who express opinions differing from their own as if it's an attack on their masculinity. As a result, they seem to be determined to put the little lady in her place. I don't have a good answer for dealing with that, I'm afraid, because I'm still learning myself."

High school administrator Elizabeth, who has a daughter nearly Tammy's age, offers counsel that has been productive for her as she has incorporated male subordinates into her team. "Try to build them up so they don't feel like you're always criticizing or harping at them," Elizabeth says. She also observes,

Most of the younger men don't have a problem, but some of the older men really do have a problem with women managers. They think they can do everything their way, no matter how much you try to get them into the circle. The only thing that works is: Over a period of time you can try to help them understand that all you're asking from them is for them to do their job. Make it clear that you're making them a part of the team—you want them to join in, contribute and work with the group.

She says the key is giving the situation time (weeks, months, sometimes years) and giving the employee freedom to make mistakes by doing things his own way until he understands that teamwork has its benefits and rewards.

Straightforward Talk

Let's return to the scene going on in my home. As I listen to the workers calling out to each other in their native language, speaking what sounds to me like gibberish, laughing aloud at jokes which (for all I know) could have my name in the punch line, I find my frustration level multiplying quickly. If I listen too long, I become angry, because as much as I wish I could understand them, I am forever trapped on the outside of their communication circle. This is how women have felt for many years in business settings where major conferences may be held not in the board room, but in the men's room. Similarly, when we're in control we may leave men out of our conversations by communicating in our own language—saying things to each other that only we insiders understand, making decisions in settings where the men may not be present.

Tammy comments,

> Anyone, but particularly a woman, needs to de-
> termine to make the effort it's going to take to learn
> what communication methods work best with dif-
> ferent kinds of people. You can have all the talent in
> the world, but if you can't relate to the people
> around you, you're not going to get very far—and
> you'll never be a leader. It goes back to what they
> taught us in journalism school: Know your audience
> and write to them. The same principle applies in of-
> fice situations—know as much as you can about the
> people you must relate to, and tailor your communi-
> cation to them.

She says that she most appreciates supervisors and coworkers—male and female—who are "up-front about what
they want, what they're doing, why they want what they
want and why they do what they do."

Holly says much the same thing when she claims,
"Women have the tendency to be too nice; we tend to bloat
our comments with qualifiers, weasel words and disclaim-
ers." She offers this example as proof of the value of the preferred method of communicating:

> I served on the school board in my community for
> fifteen years. The last time I ran for reelection, I had
> no opposition. Since I knew I would automatically
> be returned to office, I felt free to state my positions
> without softening my words for the benefit of per-
> sons who didn't agree with me. I told the commu-
> nity we needed to close the outdated (but much
> loved) high school that failed to meet safety codes. I
> said we needed to consolidate several half-empty el-
> ementary buildings, and I came out in favor of rais-

ing taxes to improve school libraries and bring computers into the classroom.

Strangely, the more honest and straightforward that I spoke, the more support I rallied. Even the newspaper applauded my "plain talk."

Holly is quick to add, however, that there is a difference between plain talk (a good thing) and blunt talk (which can be damaging and detrimental). "Every communicator has to size up her audience and know how to package her message," she says. "I cringe when I hear someone say hurtful things and excuse herself by saying, 'I was just being honest.'"

Flight attendant trainer Mary consolidates Holly and Elizabeth's observations when she says, "Part of integrity is being honest and fair with people by communicating to them ahead of time what's expected and what's not. Then, even when it comes to terminating an employee for whom the job isn't a good fit, I don't have to be nasty. I can talk to him in a way that shows that I respect him."

Esther's Communication Climax

So far, we've talked about examining our own communication patterns and watching out for the pitfalls of targeting the wrong audience or disrespecting the audience we're targeting. Now let's turn our attention toward the message we're trying to communicate.

Few of our messages are as important, as life-and-death critical, as the message that Queen Esther carried to King Xerxes. As promised, let's look at the end of Esther's story and examine how her good name, her personal restraint, her impeccable character and her skillful communication plan worked out.

Once she completed all of her courtly preparations, once she hosted the king and Haman not once but twice in her apartment, Esther finally begs the king for her life. As we saw in our first reading of the scene in chapter 9, she was straightforward in her request. "If you care about your queen, great king, spare my life and the lives of my people" (author paraphrase, see Esther 7:3). Notice, however, that she continued to exude control. She didn't spill too much information right away. Even at that pivotal moment, she didn't finger Haman.

Instead, she explained to the king why she deemed this important enough to bother him. It wasn't a matter of forced servitude, but it was a life-and-death matter. (When I hear this, I wonder about the values and decisions of this king: If he couldn't be disturbed if a whole race of people in his kingdom were to be sold into slavery, what does that say about his character?) Nevertheless, she maintained her gentle, courtly manner.

It is at that point that the king asked the question: "Who dares to threaten the life of my queen?" (7:5, author paraphrase). Only when the king's curiosity was piqued did the wise queen accuse Haman. She didn't mince words at that point. She hit Haman head-on: "The adversary and enemy is this vile Haman" (7:6). Not just Haman, but the "vile" Haman. She stopped there, though. Some of us might have been tempted to accuse the king for trusting the vile charlatan or for not knowing how his signature was being misused by his own nobles. But Esther did none of those things. She didn't try to make her husband feel guilty for the lapse in judgment. She simply spoke, with minimal accusation, to rectify the problem.

This tack turned out to be best. The king flew into a rage of righteous anger. Good stress manager that he was, he stepped outside for a walk in the garden. Just as the king turned to reenter the room, Haman threw himself at Esther's couch to beg for mercy. The king saw this, thought Haman was assaulting Esther and promptly ordered him hanged (in poetic justice, on the gallows Haman had built especially for Mordecai [7:10]). Xerxes turned Haman's vast holdings of property over to Esther, who shared the wealth with the king's newly elevated advisor—you guessed it—Mordecai (8:1-2). Together Mordecai, Esther and the king put together a new decree that entitled the Hebrew people to slaughter anyone who tried to slaughter them (8:5-11). In that way, the kingdom was purged of many Jew-haters, and God's people—even those living in the pagan city of Susa—could again live in security.

Esther's message was life-changing, her methods above reproach, and the final outcome was better than even she could have expected. By demonstrating integrity, by skillful preparation and flawless execution of her plan and especially by carefully choosing her tools of communication, Esther earned the respect of her king/husband, accomplished the freedom of her fellow Hebrews and oversaw the elevation of her beloved cousin to the position of the king's new right-hand man.

When the Message Is Life-Changing

There's one more skilled communicator I'd like us to meet. She is a teacher of the message of faith that we all carry. She is the New Testament believer Priscilla, who with her husband Aquila was a coworker with Paul and had the privilege of seeing one she discipled (Apollos) become an evangelist—a carrier of the gospel. In Acts we read:

> When Priscilla and Aquila heard [Apollos preach], they invited him to their home and explained to him the way of God more adequately.
>
> When Apollos wanted to go to Achaia, the brothers encouraged him and wrote to the disciples there to welcome him. On arriving, he was a great help to those who by grace had believed. For he vigorously refuted the Jews in public debate, proving from the Scriptures that Jesus was the Christ (18:26-28).

What did Priscilla and Aquila explain to Apollos? They explained the simple and clear message of the good news of Jesus Christ—that every individual person (male and female) has broken God's law; that the penalty for even the smallest infraction against God is ultimately death—which is a forever-after of separation from God; that rather than allowing us to remain helpless or hopeless, God's Son Jesus lived as a human and died a cruel death in our place; that by believing this and asking God to apply Jesus' death to our law-breaking account, we can be assured that we'll spend this life as His child and forever after with Him in paradise.

Despite the fact that she was speaking to a man in a culture where women's words and opinions were not valued (a woman's word was not admissible as testimony in court in that culture), Priscilla (together with Aquila) was able to communicate this all-important message with such clarity, such confidence, such believability, that Apollos was equipped not only to believe but also refute skeptics publicly and effectively.

We can learn from Priscilla that clear communication—especially when handling the life-saving message of Jesus Christ—is more than a nice skill to take out and polish up every now and then. Rather, it is a critical tool that we must hone daily if we are to be worthy of the crucial message we carry into the world.

Questions for Prayerful Consideration

1. Taking an honest self-assessment, how do I believe other people perceive my style of communicating?
2. What are two specific ways I can improve my communication skills?
3. How will I handle those individuals I encounter at work who might challenge my authority to lead or discount my opinions as I try to communicate them?
4. How have I responded to the message Priscilla communicated to Apollos? Have I made my situation right with God by asking Him to forgive me for breaking His law?

In the space provided, write in your own words the message of the good news of Jesus. Practice telling this story over and over until you feel comfortable and confident and ready to share it with everyone you meet.

_____

_____

_____

_____

_____

_____

_____

_____

_____

_____

_____

_____

_____

_____

_____

Endnote

1. Online: http://www.amazon.com/exec/obidos/tg/stores/detail/-/books/006016848X/ reviews/102-9754817-9689721#006016848x5151.

Epilogue

Holly: The Whole Truth

Once I was assigned to write a profile article of a successful Christian businesswoman. She was the "perfect woman"—happy wife, mom of two sons, owned her own business, loved to entertain, active in church . . . and the list went on.

When she explained to me how she was able to juggle so many tasks, she quickly credited a live-in nanny who shouldered the domestic half of the workload. I, as a woman and as the interviewer, was greatly relieved. She wasn't superwoman, after all! I didn't need to feel inadequate by comparison.

Of course I included the detail about her nanny in my article. But the editor took it out before publishing it. Why? "Holly," she said, "our readers can't relate to a woman who has live-in help." So in a sense the final article lied to women. We led our readers to believe this woman *was* superwoman. And since readers measure themselves against their role models, women would finish reading my article more convinced than ever that they fall short.

Honesty is a huge part of our good name. The truth is the whole truth. And integrity is telling a story truthfully, not ratcheting up the drama element or twisting information to make it fit what our superiors, colleagues or anyone else want to hear.

Putting It All in Perspective

Who may worship in your sanctuary, LORD?
Who may enter your presence on your holy hill?
Those who lead blameless lives
    and do what is right,

> speaking the truth from sincere
>   hearts.
> Those who refuse to slander others
>   or harm their neighbors
>   or speak evil of their friends.
> Those who despise persistent sinners,
>   and honor the faithful followers of the LORD
>   and keep their promises even when it hurts.
> Those who do not charge interest on the money
>   they lend,
>   and who refuse to accept bribes to testify
>   against the innocent.
> Such people will stand firm forever.
>
> (Psalm 15, NLT)

When we set out upon our journey together (just a few chapters ago, it seems), we began by examining the concepts of balance and unity as they relate to the character our lives exhibit as women in the workplace. Along the way, we've broken that ethics-driven character down to its foundational building blocks: truth and justice, restraint and credibility, loyalty and attractiveness, communication and sensitivity, listening and planning. We've learned to surround ourselves with trusted advisors and mentors who will challenge our assumptions when we are straying from the straight path, who will likewise build us up when circumstances conspire to tear us down. Now, as we conclude this examination, I'd like for us to come full circle—to return to the unifying aspect of integrity.

Read the following passage, actually a prayer from the heart of a seeker of truth:

> Send out your light and your truth;
>   let them guide me.
> Let them lead me to your holy mountain,
>   to the place where you live.
> There I will go to the altar of God,
>   to God—the source of all my joy.
> I will praise you with my harp,
>   O God, my God!

(43:3-4, NLT)

Over the last twelve chapters, I've tried to light the path and lead you to the altar of God, using the truth of God's Holy Word. I've been able to offer you light and truth only because others have done the same for me. In fact, I've introduced you to many of the women who, by using these same tools in their own journeys, have had a powerful influence upon my life—whose examples of integrity have taught me many critical lessons.

During my interviews with each of these women, in preparation for writing this book, I asked, "Please fill in the blank in this sentence: 'Integrity is . . .' " While each woman's response was valid, a few of the strongest communicators of the group offered in their definitions an insightful synthesis of the rich and complex issue of character that we've studied from many angles. Holly's answer to this question was the thought-provoking story that began this chapter; Jodi's answer was the illustration of the student she encountered when she taught English in China, which served as the launching pad of this book (pages 1-2). As we seek to put into perspective all of the concepts we've learned together, let me share a few more of those comments with you.

Ann

"Integrity is treating people honestly and equally rather than adjusting your treatment of them based on who they are or what they can do for you. When you do this, people will trust you because they know you will not try to make a name for yourself by diminishing them."

Rene

"Personal accountability defines integrity to me. It's inherent in being a healthcare professional. I see physicians and nurses taking responsibility for their actions. The responsibility is so vast. We're not there for ourselves; we're there for other people. We don't stand to gain from someone else's loss. There is no room in the medical profession for people without integrity."

Eileen

"It is easy to look the other way when someone else is doing something she shouldn't be doing. But as a Christian I am challenged by my Master's integrity not to look the other way—and instead to hold my staff members accountable for their actions. But integrity also means that I must tirelessly try to do right. As a manager, how can I tell someone else not to do something that I do myself? Without this brand of integrity, I'll become just like the world."

Tammy

"Certainly integrity incorporates the old 'honest day's work for a day's pay' adage, or not gossiping about coworkers or undercutting them to the boss or stealing ideas and passing them off as your own. But in the news industry, it also means dealing honestly and fairly with newsmakers, as well as giving the public thorough and accurate reports. When I have integrity, I bring professionalism to the office and enhance the company's reputation in the community."

Jean

"Integrity is always being honest and up-front, not having any hidden agenda. Other employees sneak around or lie. But they're going to get caught, and that will make them look bad. I feel that not compromising what I believe in is the true meaning of integrity."

Elizabeth

"Integrity is being consistent in fulfilling your obligations. I've talked with my daughters about the importance of being in God's will in their careers, and being consistent in reading their Bible, praying and going to church. But aside from telling them, I believe that modeling the behavior is at least equally as important. I would hope that I could be a good role model for them."

Christina

"Integrity is being true to yourself and being true to good Christian principles. I don't know that you could be a good

Christian and not have integrity. A lot of that is soul search-ing—first finding out who you want to be and how you can be that person. My own personal integrity is trying to do the right thing, trying to treat people the way I would want to be treated."

A Final, Personal Word

My own motivation for working each day at maintaining a lifestyle of words and deeds that are driven by integrity can be found in a memorable section of the Bible book of He-brews. After spending all of chapter 11 listing off the names of men and women of faith who saw God do mighty things on their behalf and through their servant-hearted lives, the writer of Hebrews turns the corner and faces you and me head-on. He issues this challenge, to himself and to us: "Therefore, since we are surrounded by such a great cloud of witnesses, let us throw off everything that hinders and the sin that so easily entangles, and let us run with perseverance the race marked out for us" (12:1).

Over the two-millennia-and-counting life of the Christian Church, countless believers have put their lives on the line, de-pending solely upon God's provision, clinging with tenacity to His truth, rebounding off one method of torment after another and using each occasion as an opportunity to give reason for the faith that kept them strong and vibrant. When they have been scattered to the corners of the earth during times of persecu-tion, they have simply planted new churches in their new loca-tions—carrying the gospel to people who wouldn't otherwise have heard it. When they have been forced underground by

corrupt governing regimes, they have continued to flourish—
to grow and multiply—despite every enemy tactic that would
seek their annihilation. When they have been lulled into com-
placency by a lack of opposition and a life of plenty, they have
snapped back to alertness by the thousands when challenged by
the Bible-based messages of great revivalist preachers.

These are the witnesses who, like ticket holders to Olympic
competitions, are crowding into the gallery that is observing the
life-races you and I are running. These are those whom the He-
brews passage reminds us to consider—to keep in mind—as
we live out our callings. They are watching. And, more importantly, Jesus Christ who overcame and won out over all perse-
cution, who endured the ultimate indignities and lives forever
as the champion who holds in His hands the priceless prize of
our souls, is also watching.

Keeping these witnesses in mind, it is myself I challenge
along with you as we conclude by reading the self-revelatory
and painfully honest comments of the Apostle Paul, written to
his friends in the church of Philippi: "No, dear brothers and
sisters, I am still not all I should be, but I am focusing all my energies on this one thing: Forgetting the past and looking forward to what lies ahead, I strain to reach the end of the race and
receive the prize for which God, through Christ Jesus, is calling
us up to heaven" (Philippians 3:13-14, NLT).

My sisters—my friends—let us too run with perseverance,
with truthfulness, with strength of character, with kindness and
compassion, with determination and grace, the race that is set
before us. The prize, which we'll fully enjoy for the unending
length of eternity, is worth the sacrifice.

Questions for
Prayerful Consideration

1. What are the guiding principles of my life?

2. What do I want others—those at work and those I encounter elsewhere—to see in me? What specific steps will I take to be certain that they will perceive me in this way?

3. Which elements of this study are most memorable to me? Most relevant to my own life?

4. With which aspects of integrity do I continue to struggle? What plan will I put into place that will help me to win out over temptations in these areas—so that I will be unashamed before this great cloud of overcomers that is watching me?

Cast of Characters

Ann, a corporate bean-counter, is the person most dreaded at work. Her job is to trim budgets to the barest minimum, which does not make her popular with other department heads. She has learned to sort through the emotional difficulties of not pleasing everyone as she plans prudently for outcomes in her company's and her colleagues' best interests.

Bev is a university administrator who rose through faculty ranks and proved herself unquestionably loyal and trustworthy through decades of close scrutiny by colleagues and superiors. Even when times call for her to exhibit tenacity and toughness, she is known to conduct herself with grace and evenhandedness.

Carla is a thirty-something newlywed who, despite her youth, has been entrusted by her employer with the managerial responsibility for a number of employees. Her loyalty to her employers has consistently caused Carla to rise like cream to the top in every position she has held since high school days.

Carrie was a corporate middle manager for more than a decade before starting her own fledgling company. She says she served under the best and the worst of managers (both men and women); as a manager herself, she worked to be both tough and fair to her staffers while being faithful to her employers' demands.

Christina is a divorce attorney, wife and mother. Her lessons in the workplace range from demonstrating restraint to maintaining client confidentiality to balancing her role as mother, wife and officer of the court.

Eileen is the mother of grown children and a middle manager in a large, foreign-owned corporation. She is a woman of stunning external beauty, but also one known for her truth and fairness at work, at church and at home.

Elizabeth is a high school administrator who began as an English teacher and pursued graduate degrees (she now holds a Ph.D.) while her husband provided assistance raising their two daughters (now both young professionals themselves). Through good administrations and not-so-good ones in her city's school system, Elizabeth earned the reputation of one who is credible and trustworthy.

Holly is a woman of many hats: elected chair of her local school board (well after her own children were grown and off to college), high-profile magazine editor, public relations professional and college professor. A teacher and mentor of dozens of young women coming up behind her, Holly demonstrates the needed trait of grace mixed with truth.

Jean is a forty-something professional in the travel industry. A single adult, she has learned to cultivate the special trait of being an exceptional listener as she has sought to succeed at work.

Jenny is a pediatrician, wife and mother, published writer, and the list goes on. Although she recently has scaled back her medical practice to allow her more time homeschooling her children, she continues to treat young patients who are critically ill. In Jenny we see the exceptional traits of lovingkindness, tenderness and compassion, needed in even the most professional twenty-first-century workplace.

Joan (pronounced Joanne) is the one you want on your side when you're being audited by the IRS. A CPA known nationwide for her impeccable character, Joan (although semiretired) continues to serve on governing boards for her state and the IRS region in which she lives. She has learned, through positive and negative experiences, to cultivate a small inner circle of trusted advisors.

Jodi is a single mom of a preteen daughter, an editor, a writer and a praying woman dedicated to God. Jodi challenges me whenever we meet or even chat online, to be more like Jesus in every action, every thought, every word. She is a woman whose word is her bond.

JoyAnn, now retired, returned to the workplace as an employment recruiter after her child was grown. JoyAnn approached her job as a ministry to help match people in need of employment with positions that would suit them.

Lori is still in her twenties, yet she is a respected manager in a major spa. Despite her youth, Lori already has amassed a great deal of wisdom on presenting herself with both inner and outer beauty.

Mary recently created and implemented a complex, thorough training program for her company's front-line employees. A wife and daughter of an ailing mother, Mary balances her work demands with her loyalty to her family. She has earned the right to offer counsel on managing the increasing stress load on women at work and at home.

Rene is a critical care nurse in a major teaching hospital; she is also a wife and mother of two active preschoolers. Her strength and tenacity under pressure, as well as her gentle concern for often-demanding patients, make her a credible source as we seek to sprinkle our own workplaces with gentleness and mercy.

Tammy is a respected East Coast journalist whose reliability is unquestioned by colleagues, sources and even detractors. Her insights on applying this trait in the field of professional communication are invaluable to the woman seeking to succeed with character in any field of employment.

If we may assist you in knowing more about Jesus Christ and the Christian life, or if you would like to let the author know how this book has affected your life, please write us at:

Christian Publications, Inc.
Attention: Editorial Department
3825 Hartzdale Drive
Camp Hill, PA 17011